"This story has happened and been told all over the world. In this case, Darryl Hunt, an innocent person was unjustly found guilty of a heinous crime and began serving his sentence. He was certain his innocence would be quickly found where-upon prison administrators (judges, lawyers, warden, and guards) would apolo-gize for the mistake that had been made. I was one of the many Hunt supporters who believed along with Darryl Hunt that within months, the mistake would be found and apologies would be forthcoming. The truth did come grudgingly. Almost every one lost patience and faith except Darryl Hunt himself. Nineteen-and-a-half years later, Mr. Hunt was found innocent.

The most relevant questions are in this book. They are: 'How that happened, how Mr. Hunt survived, and how the society reacted to its mistakes.' The answers are here as well. I suggest this book as an important read for every American citizen."

—MAYA ANGELOU
author of *I Know Why the Caged Bird Sings*

"At a moment when the US has the ignoble distinction of being the world's larg-est incarcerator—we have some 5 percent of the world's population but fully 25 percent of the world's prison population—here arrives the factually and morally grounded story of Darryl Hunt, whose frame up and wrongful conviction is ter-rifyingly and meticulously documented by Wake Forest's Stephen Boyd . . . In reading *Making Justice Our Business*, I am left with an overwhelming sense of awe and gratitude for Darryl's spirit and Professor Boyd's tenacity."

—ASHA BANDELE
author of *The Prisoner's Wife*

"Stephen Boyd offers a moving account of the eighteen-year-long nightmare of Darryl Hunt. A Thrown-Away-One, threatened with state execution, Hunt refused to lie to save himself and insisted that justice be done. In the faithful work of extraor-dinarily ordinary Muslims, Jews, and Christians, we see the force of divine love that wouldn't quit, and we catch a clear vision of what it takes from all of us to create a humane society where it is easier for us to truly love all our brothers and sisters."

—SR. HELEN PREJEAN
author of *Dead Man Walking*

"It is a distinct honor to endorse this important work. Scholars are often given to writing with emotional and empirical detachment about the object of their inquiry. Stephen Boyd's fresh accounting of the story of Darryl Hunt serves to re-mind us of the escalating cost of injustice in our society and the redemptive work to which all of us are called. Darryl's hard-won freedom was a watershed moment in the betterment of North Carolina and us all. *Making Justice Our Business* is equal parts ringing social critique and personal faith journey. For Darryl and for all who continue to suffer unjustly another necessary blow against the prison industrial complex has been struck."

—ALTON B. POLLARD, III
Howard University School of Divinity

Making Justice
Our Business

Making Justice
Our Business

*The Wrongful Conviction of Darryl Hunt
and the Work of Faith*

STEPHEN B. BOYD

 CASCADE *Books* • Eugene, Oregon

Cascade Books
An Imprint of Wipf and Stock Publishers
199 W. 8th Ave., Suite 3
Eugene, OR 97401

www.wipfandstock.com

ISBN 13: 978-1-60899-966-8

Cataloging-in-Publication data:

Boyd, Stephen Blake.

    Making justice our business : the wrongful conviction of Darryl Hunt and the work of faith / Stephen B. Boyd.

    xii + 118 p. ; 23 cm. —Includes bibliographical references.

    ISBN 13: 978-1-60899-966-8

    1. Trials (Rape)—Southern States. 2. Racism—Southern States. I. Title.

F264.W8 B70 2011

Manufactured in the U.S.A.

To Darryl and all those who made justice their business

and

*To Lyn, who listened as these events unfolded and encouraged me
to show the story more than tell it*

Contents

Acknowledgments

Without Professor Alton B. Pollard III's invitation to step across the racial barrier of Highway 52 in Winston-Salem, North Carolina, I likely would never have become involved in this case, and this book would never have been written. I am forever grateful for his challenge.

Likewise, the book and the events it recounts would be unthinkable without the faith, courage, and persistence of Dr. Larry Little, Mark Rabil, the Reverend Dr. John Mendez, the Reverend Dr. Carlton A. G. Eversley, Imam Khalid Griggs, and the many other community members including Dr. Maya Angelou, the Reverend Dr. Serenus Churn, and North Carolina Representative Larry Womble, of the Darryl Hunt Defense Committee, who fought so long and hard for truth and justice in this case and to whom this book is dedicated. I am grateful for their hospitality and generosity of spirit in welcoming those of us who came late to the struggle and for sharing so freely some of the stories that appear here. As for us late comers, I am grateful for the work of the Reverends Steve Angle, Kelly Carpenter, Jeff Coppage, Richard Groves, Sid Kelly, Hal Hayek, Fred Horton, Simeon Ilesanmi, Peggy Matthews, Susan Parker, Lynn Rhoades, Laura Spangler, and Albert C. Winn, as well as Chris Baumann, John Collins, and Robert "Hoppy" Elliott. We stood on the shoulders of some early participants, led by the Reverends Steve McCutchan and Hank Keating.

I am especially grateful to Regina Kellar Lane—without whose resolution and faith justice might never have been done—for reading and correcting chapter drafts, and to her husband, Scott, for his support of her then and now. I am thankful for Geoffrey Fulton's permission to recount the pain caused him and his family by other wrongful prosecutions, and for their friendship. I am indebted to my sister in the faith, Deltra Bonner, who read and commented on parts of manuscripts and knew, when I had doubts, that this book would one day see the light of day. Wendsler Nosie, Sr., Theresa Nosie, and their family of the San Carlos Apache Reservation in Arizona have been a constant source of inspiration and have taught me that justice is the business of the whole human family. The Reverend Greg Alexander, General Minister, Disciples of Christ, Kentucky offered encouragement throughout the project. The hospitality of Kent Shrader of the Mt. Shepherd Retreat Center afforded a peaceful, hopeful place to write very disturbing parts of this story.

A portion of the proceeds of this book will go to support the work of the Darryl Hunt Project for Freedom and Justice. For their work on the Staff and on the Board of Directors I thank Nigel Alston, Mary Andreolli, Tabetha Bailey, Madeline and David Harold, Angela Hattery, Terry Hines, Vernessa Wright, Darryl Little, Gene Malloy, Nelson Malloy, Walter Marshall, Reginald McCaskill, Paula McCoy, Pam Peoples-Joyner, Avon and Ben Ruffin, Jennifer Thomspon, and Wendy Morgan Butterfield Williamson.

The Reynolds Leave Program of Wake Forest University provided me with time off from teaching and other responsibilities to work on the manuscript. My thanks especially to Vice-Provost Mark Welker, whose work facilitates our own in a variety of ways. I appreciate my colleagues in the Department of Religion for creating a stimulating and congenial academic home; Jay Ford and Mary Foskett for taking on leadership roles that allowed me to complete the book; and Ulrike Wiethaus, Director of Religion and Public Engagement, for her constant support in this and other work. Thanks also to the students in the Spring 2005 REL 332 Religion and Public Life class for their lively engagement of some of this material and the panel discussion we had with the protagonists in this story.

The book would not have been possible without two outstanding journalistic sources. Phoebe Zerwick of the *Winston-Salem Journal* wrote a meticulously researched eight-part series entitled "Murder, Race, Justice: The State vs. Darryl Hunt," on the Sykes Case, a series that not only played an important role in the events narrated here, but also serves as invaluable source for any account written about them. In addition to these articles, documents, photographs and prior and follow-up news articles are archived at http://darrylhunt.journalnow.com. Thanks to Julie Harris for her work on granting me permission to use Journal photographs. Ricki Stern and Annie Sunberg produced the compelling HBO Documentary, "The Trials of Darryl Hunt," (http://www.breakthrufilms.org) and permitted the use of quotations from key figures in the film. In addition, the Sykes Administrative Review Committee compiled, sifted, and made available material related to the case. One of its members, Jet Hollander, continues to serve as an exemplar of a community member who makes justice his business. While using these and other sources, the impressions and understandings represented in the book are mine. I have tried to the best of my knowledge to report accurately what is attestable and what is hearsay and am aware that others might well differ with me.

The effort to make this story accessible to a wide audience has been a difficult one. I am deeply grateful to Ulrike Guthrie, an excellent editor and advisor, who helped me bring order, clarity, and heart to the writing and whose confidence, availability, and encouragement in this work was critical. I appreciate Charlie Collier and his colleagues at Wipf and Stock, who were struck by this story and agreed to publish this book.

I thank Lyn Warmath-Boyd who learned from her mother, Ann, that everyone deserves our loving attention, and who helped create a home in which writing this book made perfect sense.

And, finally, thanks to Darryl Hunt for his extraordinary integrity, faith, and indomitable spirit, and for helping me tell of these events from my perspective.

one

The Assaults, Murder, and Making a Case Against Darryl Hunt

THE ASSAULT OF DEBBIE SYKES

Deborah Sykes and her husband, Doug, moved to Winston-Salem from Chattanooga, Tennessee, in the summer of 1984. Having grown up in North Carolina, they were returning home. Twenty-five years old, she was a tall, attractive brunette. The evening paper hired her in July as a copy editor and headline writer. Doug worked for her uncle installing telephone equipment. They stayed with his parents in Mooresville and had just found a house complete with a nursery north of Winston-Salem and had an appointment to close on it that afternoon, Friday, August 10. Rushing to get to work by 6:00 a.m., Deborah parked her blue Opal on a side street two blocks from her office.

That morning, Willard Brown had been out all night celebrating his twenty-fourth birthday, visiting one drink house after another. By 6:30 a.m. he was looking to rob someone and saw Deborah get out of her car. Released from prison in June, Brown approached her on the sidewalk.[1]

---

1. Brown, the tenth of fourteen children, had been sent, for discipline problems, to training school four times since he was ten years old. Two older brothers and a sister were convicted felons. In 1977, he pled guilty to sixteen charges of breaking and entering,

1

Deborah Sykes. Credit: © 1984
Winston-Salem Journal photo

Willard Brown. Credit: © 1984 *Winston-Salem
Journal* photo

At 5 feet 7 inches, he was 3 inches shorter than Mrs. Sykes. He threatened her with a knife, and reached up and took her around her neck, pulling her over and toward him. Two white men driving by on their way to work noticed Brown and another black man with Mrs. Sykes on the sidewalk. A few minutes later, Brown headed toward a row of short, tarred telephone poles. When Mrs. Sykes resisted, he threw her to the ground, straddled her, and raped and sodomized her, stabbing her in the neck and upper torso as she struggled. Hearing two men on a path nearby, Brown jumped up, zipped up his pants, and ran across a field, crossed a street, ducked into an alley beside a fire station and disappeared. The two black men— Bobby Upchurch and Ralph Nash—continued on to work, assuming they had seen two drunks fighting. One of the sixteen stab wounds pierced the aorta above Mrs Sykes's heart; she died almost instantly.

Just before 7:00 a.m., a third African-American man, Johnny Gray, who police would later discover had a long criminal record in Greensboro, called 911 from a pay phone at the Black Velvet Lounge about a mile from the scene, reporting that he had seen a woman beaten. Identifying himself as "Sammy Mitchell," Gray said the assault had happened near a fire hall; unfortunately, the dispatcher sent the squad car to the wrong station.

By this time on that Friday, August 10, co-workers at the newspaper office had become worried and several walked the neighborhood looking for Deborah. Prompted by calls from the newspaper, the police sent out detectives around noon to help with the search. Around 1:30 p.m., a man

---

larceny, and larceny with a vehicle. He was in the tenth grade. He served seven years of a ten-year sentence. Wilson and Zerwick, "Marked Past."

on lunch break from a nearby knitting plant sat on the telephone pole fence eating hot dogs. He noticed a purse on the ground, with some shoes and a sweater beside it. When he reached down to pick up some change on the ground, he noticed Mrs. Sykes's body, lying on her side with blood staining her blouse and legs. Detective Jim Daulton, recently promoted, caught his first homicide case.

DARRYL HUNT AND A FRIEND MINDING THEIR OWN BUSINESS

Three miles away, Darryl Hunt, nineteen, and his friend, Sammy Mitchell, twenty-eight, woke up hung over around 7:30 a.m. in the living room of Cynthia McKey. She shared her home with her two sisters, a brother-in-law, and his five children. Darryl and Sammy had been out drinking the night before and around 11 p.m. had crashed at Cynthia McKey's—a friend with whom they occasionally stayed.

Darryl Hunt. Credit: Winston-Salem Police Department photos

Darryl had known Sammy since childhood but had grown close to him around 1982, because Sammy had known Darryl's mother, Jean. She had been shot to death in a lovers' quarrel in 1974, when Darryl was nine.[2] Because of her drug addiction, Darryl had not known Jean was his mother until two weeks before her death. The couple that raised him,

---

2. Zerwick, "Murder, Race, Justice," pt. 2.

William and Hattie Stroud, whom Darryl referred to as his grandparents, always spoke of Jean as his aunt.[3] Mr. Stroud put in thirty-eight years for the city and ended his career as a foreman in the Street Division. After Mrs. Stroud's death in 1972, Darryl and his brother helped out his grandfather around the house. Darryl was responsible for counting out and delivering the cash to pay the bills. He contributed to the household budget with money from a paper route.

After Mr. Stroud's death in 1978, Darryl and his brother, Willie, went to live with an aunt and uncle, Allie and William Johnson. Darryl worked at Steve's Italian restaurant and stopped attending school in the ninth grade. His step-sister, Juanita, invited him to visit her in Monterey, California; he lived with her for two years and worked in landscaping until he got a job in a bakery.

In 1982, Darryl received $6,380 from Mr. Stroud's estate, and he moved back home to Winston-Salem. He met a woman and spent most of his inheritance setting up an apartment for them and her newborn baby, Tahara, from a different relationship. He went to work for her father's construction business.

By the summer of 1984, Darryl had broken up with the woman, was doing odd jobs, and spent a lot of time with Sammy Mitchell. They were known in East Winston (the historically African-American part of town) as "The Blues Brothers"—Darryl slight of build with his hair in corn rows and Sammy a bit stockier and with a full beard. They frequented the Trade Street Pool Room, Service Distributors—a gas station and convenience mart near a corner where prostitutes worked—and several "drink houses"—apartments and houses where liquor was sold by the drink without state permits. Sammy had a long history of scrapes, fights, knifings, and petty theft. Darryl had three marks on his record involving trespassing and vandalism of personal property, all in the company of Sammy.

He had also developed a relationship with a young white woman, whom he called "Little Bit." When their relationship began, she told Darryl her name was Brenda Marino and that she was twenty. Soon, he discovered that she had a $200-a-day drug habit she supported by prostitution. After several arguments, he told her he would stop seeing her if she didn't get help with her addiction and stop turning tricks.

After waking up at the McKey home on August 10, Sammy had a 9:30 a.m. court appearance, so he and Darryl headed to the courthouse where

3. The Strouds had taken in Jean and her three children some years earlier.

they met Mattie Mitchell, Sammy's mother, and "Little Bit." The case was continued, so at 10:30 Darryl and Sammy walked over to the Trade Street Poolroom, where Al Kelly and Johnny Gray were also regulars. They had lunch at Mabe's Restaurant and spent the rest of the afternoon at the "Pink Apartments," where Mattie lived on Patterson Avenue.

Early in the evening, Darryl and Sammy made their way to the Service Distributor Store, where Sammy's girlfriend, Ann, often worked the streets. The clerk told them Detective Daulton had left his card and wanted Sammy to call him. She called Daulton, and Sammy walked up the street to pay a bar tab, telling Darryl to let Daulton know he'd be right back.

When Daulton arrived, he asked Darryl, "Are you Sammy Mitchell?"

"No," Darryl replied.

"That's right, Sammy's got a beard." Daulton said.

Then, "Was Sammy with you last night?"

"Yes."

"All night?"

"Yes."

Daulton asked, "Do you know if Sammy made a phone call?"

"No, Sammy didn't make a phone call. You can ask him, he's coming across the street now."

"No, that's okay, we just wanted to find out if he made a call."

Daulton waved to Sammy and drove off.

The following Tuesday, August 14, Darryl and Sammy got another card from Daulton at Service Distributors telling Sammy to come to the police station. As they walked down Trade Street toward the station, they waved down a squad car; the officer called Daulton who subsequently arrived with a tape recorder. He asked Sammy and Darryl separately whether the voice on the tape was Sammy's. Darryl laughed and said, "No, that's not Sammy."

On Friday, Darryl and Sammy went to the police station, because Sammy had been notified that he had been served a subpoena on another case. While there, Detective Daulton happened by the Sergeant's office and said he had been looking for them; he asked if they wouldn't mind talking. They said no and went upstairs and were separated. Daulton asked Darryl if he knew anything about the Sykes murder and where he was on the night of August 9. Darryl said that he knew nothing about the murder except what he had seen on the news. He said he and Sammy were at the McKeys' home, and he offered to take Daulton over to the house. Daulton declined.

JOHNNY GRAY IMPLICATES DARRYL

What Darryl and Sammy didn't know was that a major break in the case had just unraveled that day.

With unremitting pressure on the police department from the news media and citizens to find Mrs. Sykes's killer, detectives were ecstatic when Johnny Gray—the person they had been looking for since his original 911 call—called in a tip. Identifying himself as the 911-caller, Gray, accompanied by his friends Al Kelly and Gene Foster, pointed out a man in an orange jacket waiting for a bus at the corner of Fourth and Liberty Streets. That was the man that had assaulted Mrs. Sykes, he insisted. Officers stopped the bus, boarded it, and questioned a man wearing an orange jacket, named Terry Thomas. Finding marijuana in one of his pockets, they arrested him and took him to the station.

Back at the station, Detective Daulton smelled alcohol on Gray's breath but interviewed him anyway. Gray told detectives:

> I told them [when he made the 911 call], I said it was behind
> Crystal Towers by the fire station in the field. And they said they
> would check on it, so I just hung up the phone. I did do that, and
> I did recognize the man, and now if we have to come to a court of
> law to say that, I will do it, because I know this is the man I saw. I
> recognized the man [Thomas] and I'll put my life on the line that
> that man is here today.[4]

"Well, you know you'll be our witness 'cause we don't have an eye-witness to the actual crime itself," Daulton told him.

"You got one now," Gray said. "I just don't like to get myself involved. . . ."[5]

Claiming to need a place to stay, Detective Daulton gave Gray $10 and there was jubilation in the squad room. The case had been solved; they had the murderer-rapist in custody. The detectives drew up a warrant for Thomas's arrest.

4. Sykes Administrative Review Committee Report, Office of the City Manager, Winston-Salem, NC, February 2007, 38 (hereafter, Sykes Report).

5. Zerwick, "Murder, Race, Justice," pt. 2.

And then the bottom fell out. The detectives finally interviewed Thomas and told him that they believed that he had killed Mrs. Sykes. He laughed and said that he was in jail on August 10. They checked and found he was telling the truth. He could not have been the man who murdered Deborah; Gray was lying. Frustrated, Daulton, answering a press query about leads, blurted out, "I consider any black man in town to be a suspect."

What the detectives didn't know was that Gray, on the Monday after the murder, had been stopped and questioned by police on the street near the scene.[6] He didn't have identification on him and denied knowing anything about the crime. He also occasionally hung out with a large group of people at the Pink Apartments, where he stayed. The group included Darryl and Sammy from time to time; everyone played cards and drank beer. Gray was also a regular at the Trade Street Pool Room, where Officer Bob Archer had advertised the $12,000 reward for information leading to an arrest. Early on August 22, while they were drinking outside the poolroom, Gray accused Thomas of being with Hunt when he "killed that newspaper lady."[7]

The detectives subsequently discovered that Gray also used the name Johnny McConnell, had a long rap sheet, and had warrants out for his arrest in Greensboro.[8] Al Kelly, the friend who went with Gray to the station that day, said several years later that Gray wanted to collect the reward money and admitted to Kelly—and Gray's girlfriend at the time—that he had raped Mrs. Sykes during Brown's attack on her.[9] Over the next few, critical months of the investigation, Gray, despite this misidentification, became the key to the case against Darryl.[10]

August 22, the day that Gray's identification of Terry Thomas proved false, Darryl and Sammy got another card from Daulton, asking them to call. Instead, they went down to the station. When they arrived, Daulton said, "The guy [Johnny Gray] who made the 911 call just left. So we're going to interview Darryl first." Daulton then said to Darryl that they had

6. City Manager's Report, submitted by Bryce A. Stuart, Office of the City Manager, Winston-Salem, NC, November 1985, 23 (hereafter, Stuart Report).

7. Al Kelly later testified that Johnny Gray had admitted that he was involved in Mrs. Sykes's murder, as did Lisa McBride, Gray's girlfriend. Sykes Report, 68.

8. Stuart Report, 7–8.

9. Sykes Report, 68.

10. Gray was given money eight times by the Police Department, totaling $350.

someone (most likely Gray or Kelly) who could put him and Sammy at the crime scene. Daulton claimed the informant saw Darryl standing on top of the hill and Sammy at the bottom; they both were wearing black clothes, and Darryl was wearing a black T-shirt with a spider design. Daulton told Darryl that though he didn't think he was personally involved in the crime, Darryl nonetheless knew something about it. Darryl denied it and offered again to take Daulton over to the McKeys' house to verify that he and Sammy had been there at the time of the murder. Daulton again declined, but he asked Darryl if he could take his picture. Darryl agreed, and Daulton took a Polaroid picture in the interview room.

It seemed bizarre to Darryl and Sammy to be told they were somewhere they were not; that they were wearing clothes they had not worn that day (Darryl bought the black, spider-design T-shirt after the murder); and that no one would call Cynthia McKey to find out if they had actually been at her place at the time of Mrs. Sykes's assault.[11] That call wasn't made until six months later in February 1985.

TWO CONFLICTING EYEWITNESSES

The two white men who saw Mrs. Sykes on the sidewalk with two black men the morning of her murder worked at the Hanes Dye and Finishing Plant just down the street. The first, William Hooper, drove by around 6:20 a.m. and maintained that he saw one man shaking his fist in her face and the other kissing her. He never identified Hunt in a photo or live lineup and later testified that he would "bet his life" that neither of the men he saw were Darryl Hunt or Sammy Mitchell.[12] Yet he was later dismissed for being uncooperative.[13]

The second white man to see Sykes with a black man on the morning of the murder was Thomas Murphy:

> When I saw them they were leaning toward each other as if they were drunk. The black male had his right arm around her neck and was holding her right hand in his left hand, and as I went by I saw another black male about 50 feet down the street from them.[14]

11. A store clerk confirmed that t-shirts with that design were not in stock at the time of the murder. Zerwick, "Murder, Race Justice," pt. 3.

12. Petition for Commutation, 7 (2nd Trial Transcript, 1252–1262).

13. Zerwick, "Murder, Race, Justice," pt. 2.

14. Ibid.

Earlier in his life, Murphy had belonged briefly to the Ku Klux Klan and had a history of mental illness. When he heard on the news later in the day that Mrs. Sykes had been killed, he called the police. "I knew I should have stopped," Murphy told police, repeating the words between tears.[15] The police did not take a written statement from Murphy that day. But for the next several weeks, he would meet Daulton before work and sit in Daulton's car near the scene, hoping to see the man he had seen with Sykes. On August 14, Murphy misidentified Charles "Too Tall" Wall as the man down the street. Two weeks later, on August 28, while alone, he called the station, saying that he had seen the man he had witnessed holding Mrs. Sykes on the street. He described the man as 5 feet 10 inches to 6 feet tall and wearing a brown-checked shirt and light pants. When Murphy got to the station, Daulton realized that he had never taken a statement from him. In the statement Murphy signed that day—eighteen days after the murder—he used the same description for the man he saw on the street on August 28 to describe the one holding Mrs. Sykes on August 10—a man 5 feet 10 inches to 6 feet tall wearing a brown-checked shirt and light pants.[16] In the first week of September, Daulton showed Murphy a photo lineup in which one photograph lighter than the other five and had a different background. Murphy pointed to that one—the Polaroid of Hunt that Daulton had taken on August 22.[17]

AN UNSTABLE WITNESS

In an effort to determine whether Hunt might have been the person Murphy saw on August 28, Daulton left another card for Darryl and Sammy. Again, they went down to the police station. When asked where he had spent the night on the ninth, Darryl said he had spent the night with "Little Bit"—Brenda Marino. Hunt asked, again, that Daulton contact the McKeys.

Daulton located Marino, who claimed that she was with Darryl the night of August 9 and any other night he or Sammy needed an alibi. On

15. Ibid.

16. At Hunt's second trial, Murphy claimed to have seen four black men with Sykes on the morning of the murder. Zerwick, November 21, 2003.

17. Photo arrays in which one image significantly differs from the others are suggestive and, therefore, less reliable than arrays where they are the same. Wells, Small, Penrod, Malpass, Fulero, and Brimacombe, "Eyewitness Identification Procedures," cited in "Police Lineups," 3.

September 11, Daulton arrested her on old warrants for charges of larceny and failure to appear in court. In processing Marino, Daulton discovered that she also used the name Marie Crawford and was in fact a fifteen-year-old runaway from Eden, NC. She had also been an inpatient at the Forsyth County mental health facility and, according to her therapist, had a tendency to lie.[18] Daulton re-interviewed her about the Sykes murder. Since she was simply a witness, she had no right to an attorney, unless she hired one herself. None was present. "I think as a result of her being taken into custody, I know something changed," Daulton said. Crawford later said what changed was that Daulton threatened to charge her as an accessory to the murder if she did not "tell him the truth." "They just kept asking me questions," she said. "What happened to the clothes? Didn't I hide the shirt? Didn't he have blood on the shirt? That if I didn't tell the truth, I'd be charged." She then signed a statement, written by Daulton, that Darryl and Sammy had both stayed with her at the Motel 6 on Patterson Avenue on August 9, had left around 6:30 a.m. wearing dark clothing, and that Darryl had returned around 9:30 a.m. with grass stains on his pants. In addition, the statement said that Hunt had subsequently told her that Sammy had raped Mrs. Sykes. Daulton later said, "Once she was taken into custody, it was almost like, 'I needed to look after myself rather than someone else.' I think she realized she was in trouble. All she was was a runaway."[19]

Before the trial, Crawford recanted the statement.[20]

THE FOCUS SHIFTS TO DARRYL AND SAMMY

The day Crawford was arrested, Daulton showed up at the Pink Apartments looking for Darryl and Sammy. He wanted to arrest Hunt in order to have him available for a lineup for Murphy, Gray, and Hooper.[21] They

18. Sykes Report, 15, City Manager's Note.

19. Zerwick, "Murder, Race, Justice," pt. 3.

20. "Crawford has changed her story at least four times since her interview with Daulton. She recanted the two statements at Hunt's first trial. In 1986, when SBI agents and police officers re-interviewed her, she said she had not been with Hunt or Mitchell the day of the murder but had been alone on a drug binge. By 1989, she returned to a version of her original story, saying that Hunt alone came to her room the morning of the murder with blood on his right hand. Now, she says that she told police whatever they wanted to hear when they would interview her." Ibid.

21. Ibid.

were playing cards, and Daulton flashed his lights and they went over to the car to talk to him. Daulton asked Darryl how much beer he had drunk.

"About half a gallon," Darryl replied.

"Do you feel like talking?"

Darryl said, "OK," and they went with Daulton to the station. There he separated the two and began a "hard questioning" of Darryl, saying that he had witnesses that could put him at the scene of the murder. Daulton said they claimed Sammy committed the rape and murder. Darryl told him, again, that neither of them had been there. Daulton said he was lying, arrested him, and charged him with taking indecent liberties with a minor (Crawford). Another officer pulled Darryl's knit hat over his eyes and shoved him out of the room. As they were leaving, Daulton told the officer, "If you see Sammy Mitchell, shoot him."[22]

At this point in the investigation, Daulton had the statements from two witnesses—Crawford and an unidentified informant (likely Gray or Kelly) who said that the two men who attacked Mrs. Sykes had worn dark clothing. Another witness—Murphy—claimed that the murderer wore light pants and a brown, checked shirt. No one had mentioned that one of the men had a beard—a prominent facial feature of Sammy Mitchell—or had corn rows—Darryl Hunt's hairstyle at the time.

The following day, September 12, Daulton interrogated Hunt for almost three hours. He also had Hunt polygraphed, but the results were inconclusive. Though procedure at the time required a re-test, Daulton later said that the District Attorney did not want one. At 2:00 PM, Hunt was arraigned for the indecent liberties charge and the judge appointed him a public defender. Upon leaving the courtroom, Darryl was taken to the office of District Attorney Don Tisdale. When Hunt denied having anything to do with the murder, he reports that he and Tisdale had this exchange:

"You're lying. Tell us Sammy Mitchell did it and we'll let you go," Tisdale insisted.

"I don't know nothing about it."

Tisdale responded, "Look, you can have the $12,000 reward, if you just say Sammy did it." He looked at Daulton, "Isn't that right?"

Daulton said, "Yeah."

---

22. "Hunt Trial Testimony." The account of the next several days follows Hunt's testimony at his first trial. Given the events that unfolded then and eighteen years later, there seems no reason to question his account.

"I won't tell no lie for nobody or against nobody for $12,000," Darryl answered.

At that point, Daulton brought Crawford into the room, and Tisdale showed Hunt the statement she had signed about the grass stains and his implicating Mitchell.

Daulton later recalled,

> She was pleading with him (Hunt) to tell us what happened. He would talk to her and look out the window. I felt there in the office, I felt like he almost confessed. Who knows? He might have been thinking about something entirely different.

Hunt says he was quiet because they kept saying he had been somewhere he had not, and that Sammy had done something he didn't do, and that they wouldn't listen to him.

Finally, Tisdale told Hunt that if he didn't say that Sammy did it, he would put him in a lineup, and if someone picked him out, he would charge him and ask for the death penalty.[23]

Hunt left Tisdale's office and went back to the third floor of the jail while Tisdale began trying to recruit volunteers for a lineup. Since Darryl wore his hair in corn rows, he looked for people with plaited hair, but could only find one fellow inmate with braids. That afternoon, Thomas Murphy picked Darryl out of the live lineup—most likely matching his face to the earlier picture Murphy had picked out of the photo lineup.[24] The next day, September 13, Hunt stood in another lineup. This time the other inmate with braids couldn't participate, because he had misplaced his pants. William Hooper did not identify anyone in the lineup. The other witness, Johnny Gray, wrote "1–4" on a slip of paper that was entered into evidence. Darryl, whom Gray knew well, was number four and another

23. Darryl Hunt, author's interview, March 12, 2004. Also see "Hunt Trial Testimony," and Zerwick, November 18, 2003, for Daulton's assertion that Tisdale threatened Hunt with the death penalty.

24. Once a witness associates an image with the memory of a person they saw at a crime scene, the image often replaces the memory in their mind. They become convinced that they saw the person in the picture at the crime scene. Called "unconscious transfer," this can lead to eyewitness misidentification and, ironically, bolster the confidence of the witness. See "Eyewitness Identification," Kentucky Department of Public Advocacy (Online: http://dpa.ky.gov/kip/mew.htm).

random inmate was number one.[25] Gray's girlfriend later said that Gray put down two numbers to avoid picking Hunt out of the lineup.[26]

Late in the afternoon and against Tisdale's advice, Daulton applied for search warrants to obtain blood, saliva, and hair samples for testing and to search Mattie Mitchell's home, where Sammy and Darryl kept their clothes.[27]

On September 14, Daulton brought Darryl to Tisdale's office at 1:00 p.m. According to Hunt, Tisdale then walked over to a closet in his office and pulled out a stick and showed it to Hunt. He said that it was the stick that Sammy had used to beat and rob a man. After election in 1982, Tisdale had tried Mitchell for that robbery, but failed to convict him because of a hung jury.

"This is how much I want Sammy. Just tell us he did it or I'll charge you with it."

"You can't do that. I didn't do nothing."[28]

"Watch me," Tisdale said, walked over to the phone, and called down an order for Hunt's arrest for the murder of Deborah Sykes.

"WE DO NOT HAVE A SOLID PROSECUTION OF ANY KIND"

In late November, three months after Mrs. Sykes's murder, the police had Darryl Hunt in custody, but there wasn't much of a case that could be made against him. In fact, the Winston-Salem City Manager, Lee Garrity, summarizing the work of the Sykes Administrative Review Committee (2007), concluded:

> given the false statements in search warrants, Johnny Gray's iden-
> tification of Terry Thomas and subsequent identification of Darryl
> Hunt, and subsequent blood group evidence eliminating Darryl

25. A September 19, 1984, polygraph showed that Gray was deceptive when he claimed not to know Hunt and Mitchell. Sykes Report, 16.

26. Ibid., 68.

27. In the Sykes Report, the City Manager concludes that "the Mitchell apartment search warrant appears to have lacked probable cause and contained false statements" combining several witness statements in an attempt to establish all of the facts "included in the affidavit." Further, he concludes that it is unclear who actually drafted the warrant for Hunt's blood, hair and saliva and that Daulton's sworn statement "that someone identified Hunt on August 10, 1984 appears to be false." (94)

28. Interview with Darryl Hunt March 12, 2004.

Hunt as the rapist, probable cause to believe that Hunt had committed the offense did not exist.[29]

Back in August, lab work showed that the blood type of the rapist was "O" secreter. Both Darryl and Sammy were "B" secreters. The prints on Deborah's car did not match Hunt, Mitchell, or "Too Tall" Wall (whom Murphy misidentified as the second man at the scene). There was no physical evidence that linked Hunt to Sykes's murder. In addition, the eyewitness accounts did not mention one of the men wearing a beard or corn rows. The eyewitnesses, Murphy and Gray, who said they could identify the person they saw on August 10, 1984, both identified someone else before they identified Darryl. Murphy's identification of Hunt's picture came as a result of an improperly suggestive composition by Daulton that subsequently contaminated Murphy's in-person identifications. Gray's identification was tainted by his interest in the reward, his attempt to deflect police attention from himself, his failed attempt to implicate Terry Thomas, and his false denial that he knew Sammy and Darryl.

With a suspect in custody, even though they had worked closely together on the case, both the police detective and the District Attorney blamed the other for the weak evidence.

For his part, Daulton lamented that he never felt in charge of the investigation, but did what he was told.[30] He said he had been told not to put everything he had in his field notes into the reports for the file. At the first trial, he admitted having destroyed enough material in the case to fill a fifty-gallon drum.[31] After a first polygraph of Hunt scored inconclusive, the DA told Daulton that he was not interested in a second test. A minor eyewitness picked out a picture of Hunt in a photo lineup in late September 1984; the DA did not call for a live lineup until May 13, 1985.[32] When Gray failed a third polygraph on September 19, revealing he knew Sammy and Darryl, Daulton slammed his fist on his desk, "I knew he was lying." Having witnessed Tisdale's single-minded hammering on Darryl, demanding he testify against Sammy, Daulton might easily have

29. Sykes Report, 93.

30. Zerwick, "Murder, Race, Justice," pt. 4.

31. Stuart Report, 44–45.

32. Sykes Report, 16, no. 46. Given that Roger Weaver had seen Hunt's picture in the newspaper after Darryl's arrest, his identification in a photo lineup is not surprising.

concluded that the DA was more interested in convicting Mitchell than having Daulton follow up on other leads or question the ones they had.[33]

From his perspective, Tisdale expressed dissatisfaction with the investigation and the prospects of a successful prosecution. In anticipation of a probable-cause hearing for Hunt on October 31, Tisdale wrote Police Chief Masten a letter, dated October 19.[34] In it Tisdale admits feeling pressure to solve the crime—"I'm consumed with breaking this case"— and says he doesn't want an inept investigation either to cause him to have to take a "rinky dink" plea bargain or to get blamed "if the defendant must be released."[35] The purpose of the confidential letter, he says, is to see "if we can undo the damage that has been done and see that the perpetrator of Deborah Sykes' murder is prosecuted to the full extent of the law." Incredibly—given Tisdale's close contact with Daulton, including his instructions not to do a second polygraph—the District Attorney writes that he had seen the police file on the case just two days prior to his writing, on October 17.[36]

The DA had warned Daulton not to ask for a search warrant for the blood, hair, and saliva, but to go to the jail and simply take them from Hunt. Tisdale argued that to establish probable cause for the warrant Daulton would have to say there were witnesses naming Hunt. Once he did that, the witness statements and identifications would become known, increasing public attention about the case and pressure to convict Hunt. And that, said Tisdale, was precisely what happened, "Hunt has been tried in the newspaper." Because of that, Tisdale believed that if the case ever came to trial, it could not be tried in Forsyth County.

33. City Manager, Bill Stuart, concluded that the Police Department did not show proper independence from the District Attorney's Office during the investigation. Stuart Report, 44–45.

34. Masten was the Acting Chief of Police. His predecessor, Lucious Powell, had resigned in August because of conflict with the Board of Aldermen.

35. Tisdale, Letter to Chief Masten, October 19, 1984.

36. Captain G. G. Cornatzer of the Winston-Salem Police Department Criminal Investigations Division, in a memo to Major J. E. Masten dated October 29, 1984, challenged Tisdale's assertion by documenting six specific reports given to the District Attorney or interviews arranged for him with witnesses or suspects between August 22 and September 14, 1984. Exhibit IV, Sykes Report.

The problem Tisdale faced was the weak and very public evidence against Hunt and "a series of mistakes made that might very well be insurmountable."[37]

The mistakes that Tisdale seemed most concerned about were those that involved Murphy and Gray. The police had not run a background check on Murphy, did not know his history with the Klan, and allowed his guilty obsession to drive his participation in the investigation. Daulton had also not known that Gray used an alias and had an extensive criminal record.[38] Further, Tisdale found incredible Gray's claim that he plucked Mitchell's name out of thin air in the 911 call. He asserted to Masten that Gray had to know more than he was saying and that "it is imperative that we turn Mr. Gray [that is, convince him to change his testimony] and have him tell the truth." In addition, Tisdale complained that before Hunt's first lineup, he had not been informed of his right to have his attorney present, jeopardizing his testimony's admissibility in court. Further, he objected to the poor quality of the request for the search warrant for Mrs. Mitchell's apartment, saying that whatever was found might also be inadmissible.

Because of the mistakes and the weakness of the evidence, Tisdale wrote that he had to tell Deborah's family that, since "I did not find it appealing to lie to them . . . [his] most encouraging word was that we were in trouble."

Given what Tisdale had said to Darryl in the presence of Daulton on September 12 and 14 about his conviction that Sammy and not Darryl was the perpetrator, the letter to Masten appears to express his frustration that Daulton's investigation had not produced evidence against Mitchell and might build pressure for a prosecution and conviction of Hunt, against whom the evidence was weak. Tisdale seems to suggest that the solution would be for the police to get better evidence against Hunt or to find evidence that linked Mitchell to the murder. In closing, Tisdale asks Chief Masten for "whatever resources it takes to move heaven and earth" in preparation for the probable-cause hearing scheduled for two weeks later.

Four months later, Tisdale was still worried and wrote a second letter to Chief Masten on February 4, 1985. Again, he complained about too much information being released to the press. Further, Tisdale grumbled

37. Tisdale, Letter to Chief Masten.

38. Tisdale's office discovered Gray's alias, McConnell, and the criminal record under that name. This information was not shared with the defense.

that he had not received any updated reports about the matters he had raised previously, including issues with the evidence about Hunt. Because this work had not been done, Tisdale declared, "it is abundantly clear to me there is a person (or persons) at large who are responsible for the crime in question." He asked Masten to have Daulton contact Gray, Crawford, and Murphy to make appointments with him as soon as possible. Finally, he stated, "Contrary to what has been expressed publicly, we do not have a solid prosecution of any kind."[39]

Despite his pleas to the Chief, by the second week of February 1984, Tisdale had no evidence against Sammy Mitchell and nothing on any other suspect. He was worried about the flaws in the evidence against Hunt. In fact, the blood analysis came back showing that neither Darryl nor Sammy matched the blood type of the rapist.[40]

The District Attorney had a decision to make. He could let Hunt go, tell the Sykes family that, despite the headlines, Deborah's killer had not been found, and appear soft on crime to the white electorate. Or he could go forward with the prosecution of Hunt and risk others, particularly in the black community, saying that he was "knowingly trying an innocent man for his life."[41]

Tisdale chose the latter course. Despite his earlier conviction that there was not "a solid prosecution of any kind," he decided to prosecute Hunt for the murder of Deborah Sykes. He asked for the death penalty.[42] Momentum in the DA's office and the police department built that spring for the trial that began on May 28. It was momentum that would serve to mask another—perhaps three other—violent sexual assaults by Willard Brown.

39. Don Tisdale, Letter to Chief Masten, February 6, 1985, www.journalnow.com, Documents.

40. Hunt's test results were known in November 1984; Mitchell's came back March 11, 1985. Sykes Report, 5–6.

41. This is the assessment of Michael Grace, the current law partner of Don Tisdale. Zerwick, "Murder, Race, Justice," pt. 4.

42. Of this decision, Tisdale later said, 'You never have a perfect case; you'd love to have a perfect case. You'd like to have the pieces fit, but they just don't ever fit that way " Stern and Sunberg, *Trials of Darryl Hunt*, 18:13–18:29.

THE ASSAULTS OF REGINA K., LINDA E., AND KATHLEEN D.

When the results of the blood analysis on Darryl came back in November 1984, the police knew that they did not have the rapist in custody.[43] As far back as August 29, 1984—the day after Gray's identification of Terry Thomas proved false—Lt. Jerry Raker, a Lieutenant in the Criminal Investigation Division, admitted that they had no leads, despite Daulton's continued attempts to milk more information from Gray and Thomas Murphy. Lt. Raker said he thought that they should be looking for someone with a history of violence. To Tisdale, "it was abundantly clear" that the rapist/murderer of Mrs. Sykes was still at large. Indeed, Willard Brown was at large and still very criminally active.

On February 5, the day before Tisdale's letter, the *Winston-Salem Journal* carried a story of a vicious rape of a nineteen-year-old woman, Regina Kellar, who was abducted two blocks from the scene of Deborah's assault—a connection mentioned by the writer.[44]

At 7:45 a.m., having parked in a small lot on Poplar Street, Regina walked across the street to a side entrance of the Integon Insurance building where she worked. She was stopped by a black man she later described as being about 5 feet 6 inches tall and wearing a hooded sweatshirt. He put a gun to her side and said, "You don't need to make a move; you don't need scream. You need to turn around and walk back to your car."[45] With his other arm, he grabbed her around the neck and pulled her over toward him. At gunpoint, he forced her back to her car and told her to drive. They stopped at a wooded area near an apartment building just outside of downtown. He took $300 from her purse and her watch. He told her to take off her clothes. He awkwardly raped her in the backseat of the car, then pulled her out and tried to enter her from behind. She resisted him by twisting and turning, so he put the gun on the top of her car. She grabbed it and turned it on him and pulled the trigger twice. It didn't fire. He pulled a knife and took the gun from her, "You stupid bitch, it's empty, but I've got a knife that will kill you." With that he spun her around

43. City Manager, Sykes Report, 93.

44. Regina Kellar married May 11, 1985 and changed her name to Regina Kellar Lane. She is referred to throughout the newspaper reports and police documents as Regina K.

45. Stern and Sunberg, *Trials of Darryl Hunt*, Special Features, HBO Featurette, Exclusive Interview with Regina Lane, 2:22–2:26.

and put the knife to her throat. She lowered her chin so he couldn't cut her jugular vein. The second time he tried to cut her throat, she wrapped the fingers of both hands around the blade. Wearing gloves, he reached around her head and grabbed the middle of the knife, and they struggled for control. Both fell on the gravel; she was face down with him on top of her. Holding the knife with one hand, he reached down, picked up a shard of broken glass, and tried to slit her throat. On her knees and elbows, she pushed up and twisted, until they were standing facing each other. He told her she needed to let go of the knife and was going to count to three. She responded, "You're crazy if you think I'm going to let go of this knife so you can kill me." He counted anyway, and, on three, she pulled for all she was worth, took the knife, and started running.[46] Naked and bleeding from twelve stab wounds, Regina ran about half of a mile and pounded on doors until a middle-aged African-American man named David Wagner took her in, covered her, and called the police.[47]

Though there was a lot of blood, all of it was Regina's. However, responding officers recovered the knife, one of the gloves worn by the assailant, discovered footprints of a man wearing tennis shoes, and saw the direction in which he headed. Detective Bill Miller, who assisted Daulton in the Sykes case, began the investigation, with the help of Detective Mike Barker. Regina K. officially described her attacker as wearing a hooded sweatshirt, being between 5 feet 7 inches and 5 feet 9 inches tall, about 120 to 125 pounds, and around twenty-five to thirty years old. Since they had the perpetrator's glove and knew the direction he had fled, Regina's fiancé, Scott Lane, asked that the officer call in hounds to track him. The police rejected the suggestion, saying that the rainy conditions would impair the tracking. Miller's initial report omitted any mention of the perpetrator pulling Ms. Kellar down and over toward him, although she asked him several times to include it.[48] Detectives and officers canvassed the area and questioned the driver of a bus for which a pass had been left

46. Interview with Regina Kellar Lane, January 6, 2011.

47. Regina Keller Lane, interview by author, June 15, 2009.

48. Keller Lane interview, January 6, 2011. Later, she realized that Mrs. Sykes's rapist had done the same thing and felt that he would appear taller than he was, leading witnesses in the Sykes case to be mistaken about his height. She stressed the importance of this point later to the Sykes Review Committee in 2006. In addition, Miller did not accurately report that, while she had been raped inside the car, she resisted his attempts when he pulled her outside and did not simply do everything he told her to do.

at the scene. Two days later, Detectives Miller and Barker drove Regina around the areas where she had been abducted and assaulted looking for the perpetrator, to no avail.

On February 7, Regina asked Miller whether the same person who assaulted her might have assaulted Mrs. Sykes. He left the room and returned with a picture of Darryl Hunt and Sammy Mitchell, asking her if either of them had been her attacker. She said no, but pressed him on a possible connection with the Sykes murder. She reported that he responded by saying, "We don't want anything to hurt our case against Darryl Hunt."[49] On May 15, Regina's case was given to Detective Carter Crump. On May 23, Regina identified Willard Brown's photo as someone who resembled her attacker. Detective Daulton also signed this report. Shortly before Hunt went on trial, Regina asked Crump whether it might be the same person who killed Deborah Sykes. He responded by saying that Brown couldn't have attacked Mrs. Sykes, because he was in prison. For the next eleven months almost nothing happened; Crump filed reports saying that he couldn't find Brown. Then, in March 1986, Brown was arrested on another charge. Crump interviewed Brown and asked him, surprisingly, not about the rape of Regina K., but about the Sykes murder. Brown denied any involvement and said that he was in prison on August 10, 1984, the date of Mrs. Sykes's assault.

On April 1, Regina K. picked Brown out of a live lineup. Again, she said that he looked most like the man who attacked her. Curiously, Crump executed a warrant to take blood, hair, and saliva samples from Brown. This was odd because there was no biological evidence from the assailant left at the scene or on Regina K. to which to compare Brown's samples. Also curious is the fact that whatever Crump said in his affidavit to justify taking the samples is unknown because the warrant is no longer in any of the case files.

The lab results showed that Brown's blood type was "O" secreter—the same type as the person who raped and murdered Mrs. Sykes—six months earlier and two blocks away. In addition, the Criminal Investigation Division knew that neither Sammy nor Darryl was an "O" secreter. The pattern of twelve knife wounds about the head, neck, and upper torso on Regina K. resembled the sixteen on Deborah Sykes. Regina K. had identified Brown in a photo and live lineup, and Crump had interviewed Brown about the Sykes murder just a month before. The connection to the Regina

49. Ibid.

K. assault also established a pattern of violent, sexual assault by Brown. As Lt. Jerry Raker had said back in August of 1984, whoever killed Mrs. Sykes had a history of violence—something many other detectives would have assumed upon first examining the Sykes crime scene. Finally, both Regina Kellar and Deborah Sykes were abducted in a similar way, with the assailant pulling them down and close to him, distorting perceptions of his height and giving the appearance that the two were intimate; unfortunately, this last information was not recorded in the file.

This is what Crump and others in the CID knew in May 1986, almost a year after Darryl Hunt's conviction. One would think that Detective Crump would have made that connection in the spring of 1986. This is especially true when one considers the other major assignment Crump had at the time. He was the WSPD liaison for the State Bureau of Investigation (SBI) of the Sykes murder (January 1986–October 1986).[50] He would have been going over the autopsy reports and material evidence, including the lab reports on the blood. But he later said he didn't make that connection.

When Regina K. specifically asked about a connection in May 1985, with Hunt's trial a week away, Crump said that Brown couldn't have attacked both women, because he was in prison when Sykes was assaulted. By May 1986, Crump had interviewed Brown and was deep into reviewing the evidence concerning the Sykes murder. In 2003, and again in 2005, he said three different things about what he thought in May 1986 about Brown's possible involvement in the assault on Mrs. Sykes. First, he said that he believed Brown was *not* in prison, but that he didn't know of any evidence that would link him to the Sykes murder. And yet there was, of course, Brown's blood type, the wound patterns, the choice of weapon, and proximity of time and place of the attacks. Further, a new witness, Kevey Coleman, may have identified Willard Brown as one of the two men he saw with Mrs. Sykes the morning of her murder.[51] Second, a month later, Crump said that he did make the connection, but he be-

50. See chapter 2, below. The City Manager, Bill Stuart, after doing an administrative review demanded by citizens, requested a re-investigation of the Sykes murder by the SBI.

51. Coleman came to the attention of the SBI investigators due to a call to the CrimeStoppers line on May 21, 1986. Coleman reported that he was on his way home the morning of August 10, 1984, and saw two black men with a white woman he later identified as Deborah Sykes. In a 2005 interview, Coleman said that, when he identified Willard Brown as one of those men, the SBI agent and WSPD Detectives Crump and Riley Spoon argued that Brown could not have been involved, because he was in prison at the time. See chapter 2.

lieved that Brown *was* in prison on August 10, 1984, the day of Sykes's murder. That is what Brown had told him March 12, 1986. Third, in 2005, Crump further claimed that he hadn't just taken Brown's word for that; he had checked with the Department of Corrections. There is no report in either the Regina K. or Sykes case files to document that he actually did so.[52] In fact, Ms. Kellar reports that she explicitly asked Crump for documentation from the DOC that proved Brown was in prison and that Crump refused to provide it, telling her that she would just have to take their word for it. Seventeen years later, when Detective Rowe checked the Department of Correction records, he discovered that Brown had not been in prison on the day of Deborah Sykes's murder; he had been released on June 13 or 14, 1985.[53]

Or maybe Crump did make the connection and came to suspect, in 1986, that Brown had killed Mrs. Sykes. That could explain why he would ask Brown about the Sykes murder rather than the Regina K. rape in the March 12 interview. Brown gave Crump his alibi; he claimed to have been in prison. It also could explain why Crump ordered a lab analysis of Brown's blood when there was no biological evidence in the Regina K. case to compare it to. However, if Crump did believe that Brown murdered Sykes, why didn't he take that to his superiors and the DA and, if he did, why wasn't the investigation re-opened?[54] The possibility that Willard Brown raped and murdered Mrs. Sykes would have unraveled the case made against Hunt the year before, embarrassed the police department and DA's Office, and opened the city to civil liability. This may explain why there are key documents missing in the case file of Regina K.

Mark Rabil, Darryl's attorney, later said that if the police department didn't know in 1986 and at Darryl's second trial that Brown was *not* in prison the day of Deborah Sykes's murder, it was negligent, and if it did know, it was criminal.[55] Information about the Regina K. assault and her identification of Willard Brown were never shared with any of Hunt's attorneys.

52. Sykes Report, 56. These various statements were made to Detective Mike Rowe in December and January of 2003 and in informal conversations with the Sykes Review Committee investigators in 2005.

53. See chapter 4.

54. Since Crump refused to be interviewed by the Sykes Administrative Review Committee, it is difficult to reconcile the various things he has said about this matter and to understand why he did some of the things he did.

55. Stern and Sunberg, "Trials of Daryl Hunt," 1:27:43–53. See chapter 5.

After Regina K. identified Brown in the live lineup on April 1, 1986, she asked Crump to do a voice identification lineup to make absolutely sure he was the man who attacked her. (Because Brown had worn the sweatshirt's hood over his head, she hadn't seen his hair or chin and so was not absolutely certain about her identification.) On May 20, Crump asked her for a list of words her attacker had said. On that same day, a man called the CrimeStopper line saying that Kevey Coleman had been a witness to the Sykes assault. Crump was among the detectives who interviewed Coleman two days later; in that interview, Coleman identified Willard Brown as one of the men he saw with Mrs. Sykes on the morning of her murder. He reports later that the detectives informed him that he must be mistaken, because Brown was in prison at the time.[56] On July 6, Crump informed Ms. Kellar that, after talking to the Public Safety Attorney, a decision was made not to do a voice identification lineup.[57] Had Regina Kellar been allowed to participate in a voice lineup and had that resulted in her being certain that Brown was her attacker and had she decided to go forward with the prosecution, the similarities between the two cases would have become more public and may have cast "doubt on Hunt's guilt." That could have opened the city to a liability claim by Hunt, had he been exonerated as a result.

By February 1987, Brown was in prison on another charge. When Crump went to interview him and Brown invoked his right to an attorney, Crump left. Two months later, Crump called Regina and asked her to take the weekend to consider whether she wanted to go through with the prosecution of Brown. In that conversation, she reported that Crump told her that, without any physical evidence, it would be her word against his. If he were convicted, he would probably be sentenced to only three to five years on the rape, kidnapping, and robbery charges. She reiterated a request she had made of Miller in 1985—that attempted murder be added to the charges, as her attacker tried several times to slit her throat. Miller had responded that, since the gun was not loaded, the charge could not be added. Crump said that, because the charge had not been added during the investigation, it could not be added now. She also asked Crump if Brown had a gun charge on his record. She reports that Crump said

56. Sykes Report, 55.

57. The Public Safety Attorney at the time, Claire McNaught, later testified that she had no memory of that conversation or any discussions of the possible prosecution of Willard Brown in the Regina K. case. Sykes Report, 56.

that he did not. Department of Corrections records, however, reveal that Brown had served time in 1982 on a charge of "possession of a firearm by a felon."[58] He reported that she decided not to go forward. Today, Regina Kellar Lane says that she didn't go forward because the police would not schedule the voice lineup that would have helped her be certain she had identified the right man.[59] In addition, there was physical evidence, including the knife she wrestled from her assailant, which could have been used at the trial.[60] On September 10, 1989, the case was finally closed.

In a six-month period before and after Mrs. Sykes's murder, two other strikingly similar sexual assaults took place within a few blocks of the fence where Brown had left Deborah Sykes.

LINDA E.

On June 13, 1984, the day we now know that Brown was likely released from prison, a black male approached Linda E. and stuck a gun in her back, saying, "You have to come with me"—similar to what the perpetrator would say to Regina K. eight months later.[61] For the next seven hours, the man dragged Linda E. over a four block area forcing her to fellate him and raping her vaginally five times. After the last rape, he left her behind the fence, not two hundred yards from where Mrs. Sykes would lie two months later. Linda E. described her assailant as 5 feet 3 inches, about 120 pounds, twenty-five years old, with a mustache and beard. She also said

58. Stern and Sunberg, "Trials of Darryl Hunt," Regina Lane featurette, 20:03–20:25.

59. At the time, Ms. Lane said she was 80–85% certain Willard Brown was her assailant. That was not enough, in her mind, to prosecute him. In addition to the voice recognition lineup, it would have been helpful to know whether Brown assaulted Mrs. Sykes in the same way six months before. Since Detectives Miller and Crump insisted, without showing her documentation, that Brown was in prison at the time of Mrs. Sykes's murder, they led her to believe that Sykes' attacker could not have been hers. Further, given Crump's assertion that Brown's conviction would have resulted in a sentence of three to five years, she did not think it worth going through a trial. In fact, under sentencing guidelines in effect at the time, if convicted of first-degree rape and kidnapping, Brown would have been sentenced to life in prison for each charge. The robbery charge would have brought 20–40 years.

60. See chapter 5, n. 2.

61. It is a bit unclear exactly when Brown was released. Lt. Joseph Ferrelli, who worked on the Sykes Review in 2006, believed that he might have gotten out on June 13, saying that the prison records "aren't completely accurate." He was clearly free when Deborah Sykes was murdered and may have have been free when Linda E. was assaulted. Zerwick, "Rape victim tells her story."

that he wore a large silver ring on his left hand. Detective Teresa Hicks was assigned the case on June 15 and called Linda E. but reported she did not reach her and left on vacation. Hicks finally interviewed Linda E. on June 26 and had her take a polygraph, which Linda passed, on July 3. Hicks noted ten days later that she had checked the neighborhood unsuccessfully for someone matching Linda's description. Hicks stopped working on the case because of her workload. On August 2, Linda E. identified a "possible" suspect from the book of mug shots, but she wasn't sure and wanted to see a more recent picture and a live lineup. The suspect was 5 feet 10 inches and was known to Hicks from a previous assault case involving him for which she prepared a prosecution. On August 10, Hicks was called to the Sykes scene; colleagues asked her about a possible connection to the Linda E. case. It is unknown what she said that day. Later, Hicks said that there was already a suspect in the Linda E. case, and he didn't match the description of the suspect by the witnesses in the Sykes murder; those descriptions said the suspect was over six feet tall. On August 24, Hicks obtained a more recent photograph of the suspect and Linda picked it out of a photo array, but said she wanted to see a live lineup. In her reports, Detective Hicks wrote that she was never able to find the suspect for the live lineup.[62] Inexplicably, the material evidence from Linda E.'s assault—which had never been tested—was destroyed while Hicks was still looking for the suspect. Linda's clothing rape kit was destroyed on August 15—before Hicks had even obtained a more recent photo of the suspect—and the clothing itself on September 8.[63] Normally, investigators wait to send forensic evidence to the lab until there is a suspect against whom to compare the results. In this case, the evidence was destroyed before the suspect was apprehended. On September 12, Hicks discovered that Linda E. had moved out of town and left a message with her mother for Linda to get in touch with her. On October 16, 1985, Hicks curiously closed the case, writing that Linda E. had not left a forwarding address or phone number. Linda E. later said that when she learned in

62. See Linda E.'s case file, Appendix 7 of the Sykes Report.

63. Hicks does not record this in the file. During the Sykes Review in 2006, documentation indicated that Officer A. T. Stover, who took Linda E.'s initial statement, signed the order to destroy the rape kit. When questioned, Stover said he did not understand why he would have authorized the destruction of the evidence as the case was assigned to Hicks. Hicks refused to answer questions by the Sykes Review Committee about the Linda E. and the Deborah Sykes cases.

September that the evidence had been destroyed, she assumed the case was closed and saw no reason to contact Hicks.[64]

KATHLEEN D.

Five months after Deborah's assault and a month before Regina K.'s—in January 1, 1985—a black male started following Kathleen D. several blocks from the Sykes murder scene. When she got to Brunson Elementary School, he pulled a mask over his head, grabbed her, and put a knife to her throat. He tried to rob her, but she had no money in her purse. He then used the knife to rip her clothes off and forced her to fellate him. He then bent her over and raped her. When he was finished, he tied her up with her own clothes and left. She fled to a nearby apartment building for help. Again, Hicks was the investigating detective.

Kathleen D. described the attacker as 5 feet 3 inches, very thin, wearing a white sweatshirt.[65] On May 14, she was shown mug shots of men fitting the general description, but none looked like her attacker. Regina K. identified the photo of Willard Brown the following day. No police documents report that Kathleen D. was ever shown Brown's photo.[66] The case was closed.

There was, in the months leading up to the trial of Darryl Hunt in May 1985, "compelling evidence" that Willard Brown also raped Regina K., Linda E., and Kathleen D.[67] The assaults happened in the same vicinity with the same weapons, and involved the same sexual acts and the same general suspect descriptions. The perpetrator was a black male attacking white women in public locations. Had the police and the DA's Office not focused attention so obsessively on Sammy and Darryl, perhaps connections between the cases of Linda E. and Mrs. Sykes might have been made and Brown apprehended before the attacks on Kathleen D. and Regina K. Had the police made connections between and among all of the cases of Linda E., Kathleen D., and Regina K. to the assault of Mrs. Sykes, those cases may have constituted exculpatory evidence showing "a pattern of

64. In 1996 and 2003, Linda E. made contact with the Police Department and the *Winston-Salem Journal*. Due to media coverage of the Sykes case (see chapter 2), she—as had Regina—believed that the person who raped Deborah Sykes may well have assaulted her. See Zerwick, "Rape victim."

65. Her statement cannot be found in the case file. Sykes Report, 18, n. 63.

66. Ibid., 20, n. 88.

67. Ibid., 5.

rapes likely committed by someone" other than Hunt.[68] But no such connections were made. Or, if they were, they were not entered into the case
files, making them unavailable to Hunt's defense under discovery rules.

LARRY LITTLE AND THE DARRYL HUNT DEFENSE COMMITTEE MAKE DARRYL THEIR BUSINESS

In the spring of 1985, a movement was growing—primarily in the black
community—that raised questions about the case against Darryl and the
police department's handling of it. The Darryl Hunt Defense Committee
began thanks to Larry Little, a black thirty-four-year-old Alderman who
had earlier started the only North Carolina chapter of the Black Panthers.
He had seen Darryl's picture in the paper the day after he was arrested.
Little had played basketball with Hunt at the YMCA and wondered
whether the gentle, soft-spoken Hunt could do what he was accused of.
He went to see Darryl in jail and told him, "If you did this, I will help
them put you away. If you didn't, I'll help you." Darryl said, "I didn't," and
ended up owing his life to Little.

After checking with contacts in the police department, Little learned
that the evidence was flimsy. Several things bothered him. Those in the
black community who knew Johnny Gray said that he was no Good
Samaritan and that if he was involved it was probably because he had
something to do with the crime. The artist's drawing based on interviews
with Hooper and Murphy showed a light-skinned black man; Hunt was
dark-skinned. Descriptions from the interviews also said the attacker
was taller than Sykes; Hunt was shorter. Little also knew that the black,
spider-design T-shirt had been seized from Mattie Mitchell's apartment.
The warrant said that witnesses said the assailant was wearing that T-shirt
on August 10. Neither Hooper nor Murphy had mentioned that in their
statements and Darryl told Little he bought it after the crime and just
before his arrest. The clerk at the store confirmed that the T-shirt had not
been in stock at the time of the murder. Little also talked to Gray about
his story, and it didn't add up.

Little met with Gordon Jenkins and Mark Rabil, Hunt's white, court-
appointed attorneys. They asked Little if he could raise money for a private investigator. He agreed and started speaking at African-American

---

68. Ibid.

churches and held several rallies at Lloyd Presbyterian Church, just down the street from the Pink Apartments, where Mattie Mitchell lived.

Rabil grew up in Winston-Salem and observed:

> It's the archetypal situation in the South. It is the most taboo thing for a black man to do, to possess a white woman. It was the ultimate challenge to white authority. I knew from growing up here that there was racial prejudice in our county, our society and in our court system. So all of that added up to a very bad and difficult situation for Darryl.

Historically, much less of an offense than this got black men lynched. For many African-Americans in the city, Hunt became a symbol of the systemic racism and injustice they encountered every day. These feelings were fueled when the private investigator discovered Murphy's history with the Klan. As Maya Angelou said at a rally:

> We must remember that Winston-Salem is down South, but New York City is up South. Darryl Hunt exists in San Francisco, in Paris, in London, and you know how many there are in South Africa. A case can be built here on any person founded on lies and hate that can send us to the gas chamber or the electric chair.[69]

The city was divided about the case. By the time the trial started in May 1985, a survey of people called for jury duty showed that 90 percent of African-Americans thought Hunt was innocent, while 70 percent of whites believed him guilty.[70] Two new black pastors, Reverend John Mendez and Reverend Carlton A. G. Eversley, also provided leadership to the Defense Committee. Several white clergy and lay people attended rallies and contributed money. On the first day of the trial two hundred protesters marched from Lloyd Presbyterian to the Hall of Justice carrying "Free Darryl Hunt" signs and wearing similar buttons on their shirts. They were incensed and took to the streets—one of the most effective strategies inherited from the Civil Rights Movement twenty years before.

69. Zerwick, "Murder, Race, Justice," pt. 3.

70. Ibid., pt. 4.

two

Convictions and Appeals Fall
on Deaf Ears

THE FIRST TRIAL

Given the racially divided nature of the Forsyth County jury pool, both sides knew that jury selection was going to be critical to the final outcome of the trial. Jenkins and Rabil presented the judge with affidavits from other defense attorneys, testifying that District Attorney Don Tisdale had used his jury dismissals to excuse black jurors. The judge denied their motion to prevent him from doing so and jury selection began. Of the eleven blacks in the pool, Tisdale excused ten, leaving only one black juror, although Forsyth County was 25 percent black.

The prosecution's case turned on the testimonies of Thomas Murphy, Johnny Gray, and Marie Crawford. Murphy, after having misidentified the second man he said he saw the morning of Sykes's murder, now was dead certain that Hunt was the man he had seen holding Sykes. As for Johnny Gray, the second man testifying, despite his criticism of Gray's credibility, DA Tisdale had Gray arrested on March 12 for common law robbery—perhaps to make sure Gray was available to testify against Hunt. Gray denied ever having identified Terry Thomas, claiming the police had pulled the wrong man off the bus. He pointed at Darryl and

29

said, "That is the man I saw that morning attack that lady." After his testimony, he was released from custody. In September 1985, Tisdale dropped the robbery charges against him. Over the course of the process, the police paid Gray a total of $365 for his trouble.[1]

As for Marie Crawford, the third person testifying, she recanted the statement that Daulton had written and she had signed, saying that Sammy and Darryl had stayed with her the night of August 9, left at 6:30 a.m., and that Darryl had returned later with grass stains on his pants. Undeterred, Tisdale, addressing Crawford on the stand, asked her, "Did you not sign a statement on September 11, 1984 stating that. . . ." and then proceeded to read into the record line by line the very statement she had recanted! Prompted by Tisdale, Crawford also said that Little and Hunt's lawyers had visited her in jail. Her testimony suggested that the defense "acted improperly."[2] Consequently, during the trial, Tisdale asked that the State Bureau of Investigation investigate Little for witness intimidation. In the media, Tisdale excoriated Little for impersonating an officer and intimidating witnesses.

Detective Daulton denied that anyone but Hunt had ever been identified by a witness, denied paying Johnny Gray for his cooperation, and admitted destroying material on the case that he claimed was irrelevant. The private investigator for the defense had discovered from Gray's girlfriend that he had identified two people in the lineup and written "1–4" on the slip of paper. Rabil cross-examined Daulton.

"Detective Daulton, you have testified that Mr. Gray identified Mr. Hunt in the lineup on September 13, 1984. Is that correct?"

"Yes."

"But, Detective Daulton, look at this piece of paper, it has two numbers on it." Rabil said.

Daulton said, "Well, that means that the number one suspect is number four."

The courtroom burst into laughter. Reverend Eversley reported that Tisdale blurted out towards Daulton—at a volume that he and others in

---

1. Small payments to Gray were made over a twelve-month period stretching from August 22, 1984, to August 19, 1985. After the trial, Tisdale wrote a letter arguing that Gray had been an uncooperative witness and should not receive any of the reward money. Gray didn't.

2. Zerwick, "Murder, Race, Justice," pt. 4.

the gallery could hear—"I told you how to testify; now you've blown the whole damn thing."[3]

Johnny Gray was called to the stand and claimed that—on the day of the lineup—he had meant what Daulton said.

The defense then called witnesses to challenge state witnesses. The police artist testified that neither Murphy nor Hooper had described the perpetrator as wearing corn rows—Hunt's hairstyle at the time of the murder. An expert witness testified that the Polaroid of Hunt with a different background would have called undue attention to it during Murphy's initial identification. Gray's credibility was questioned, because he had first identified Terry Thomas.[4] Sammy Mitchell was called to substantiate Hunt's alibi.

Caption: Sammy Mitchell testifies. Credit: © 1985,
Winston-Salem Journal photo by Chuck Eaton

Despite threats, Mrs. Jo Anne North, a white woman and Darryl's sixth-grade teacher, appeared as a character witness. Despite repeated objections from the Assistant District Attorney, she testified that she believed Hunt to be an honest and peaceful person.[5] Finally, Darryl was called to the stand.

3. Carlton A. G. Eversley, interview by author, December 21, 2010.

4. Zerwick, "Murder, Race, Justice," pt. 4.

5. See *Long Time Coming*, told by Jo Anne North Goetz and written by Leigh Somerville McMillan, 62–65. The day of her testimony, Ms. Goetz reported that she found a note on her car that read, "Go home nigger lover." She had also received anonymous telephone calls.

Caption: Darryl Hunt (l) and Mark Rabil (r) during the first trial.
Credit: ©1985 *Winston-Salem Journal* photo

Rabil asked him, "Did anybody in the [District Attorney's] office offer you anything if you would say Sammy Mitchell did it?"

Hunt responded, "Yes, Mr. Tisdale's exact words were we can get— you can get the $12,000 if you just say that Sammy Mitchell did it and he looked at Daulton and said ain't that right, and Daulton shook his head yeah."

Rabil: "What did you say in response to that?

Darryl: "That I wouldn't tell no lie for nobody or against nobody for $12,000."[6]

In his closing argument, anticipating the defense, Tisdale argued about the presumption of innocence: "Let's understand what it means. If I am accused of a crime, I want the presumption of innocence. But [pointing at Hunt] it doesn't apply to the guilty."

As the jury recessed for its deliberation, Reverend Eversley called his wife, a professor at Wake Forest's Law School, "Baby, there's no way they can convict him on this evidence. One witness is a Klansman, another is a criminal and liar, and the third is a fifteen-year-old addict and prostitute."[7]

The jury was split from the beginning, with seven voting for guilt, five for innocence. After three days of deliberation, the jury returned a guilty verdict on June 14, 1985. Two jurors agreed to vote for guilt

6. "Hunt Trial Testimony," 1819–20.

7. Panel Discussion in Religion 332: Religion and Public Life, November 8, 2005.

provided the others would not impose the death penalty. Malcolm Ryan, the foreman, said later,

> It's a wrenching experience, especially in a case like this that was all circumstantial. There was very little evidence. Overall it was beyond a reasonable doubt, but it was not absolute. None of us were willing to sentence someone to death if we were not absolutely sure.

During the sentencing phase, there wasn't a single vote for death, because, Ryan said, "there were too many lingering doubts about Hunt's guilt."[8]

DISBELIEF, REVIEW, AND APPEAL

About seventy-five Hunt supporters attended the fourteen-day trial, and the verdict devastated them.

Hunt supporters at the trial. Credit: © 1985 Winston-Salem photo by Chuck Eaton

Prepared for the possibility of a violent reaction to the verdict, the Winston-Salem Police Department posted thirteen uniformed officers in the courtroom and as many as one hundred in the Hall of Justice and on downtown rooftops.[9] Disappointed and angry, members of the Hunt Defense Committee and other supporters went to Lloyd Presbyterian Church. In tears, Little told the crowd, "I'm going to cry all I can and

8. Zerwick, "Murder, Race, Justice," pt. 4.
9. Cone, "Hunt convicted in newswoman's murder."

then I'm going to get up on my feet and go and do more battle. We can't let this man stay in prison."[10]

Larry Little outside courtroom. Credit: ©1985 Winston-Salem photo by Chuck Eaton

And battle they did. They raised money, held rallies, and planned marches to keep Darryl's cause in the public eye.[11]

Complaints poured into the City's Board of Alderman. One of its members, Vivian Burke, asked Reverend Leonard V. Lassiter Jr., pastor of Grace Presbyterian Church, to draw up a list of questions people had about the investigation.

The "Lassiter Letter" guided a four-month Administrative Review by City Manager Bill Stuart. Stuart found that Johnny Gray should have been investigated more thoroughly as a suspect and a witness, observed that there were conflicting reports about whether Gray identified Terry Thomas, and identified three instances where the District Attorney's Office seemed to have taken over the investigation.[12] The City Manager referred the report to the Police Chief, recommending an investigation by Internal Affairs and the SBI into possible police misconduct.

The SBI and Police Department concluded their joint re-investigation with a three-thousand-page report in November, 1986. A judge

10. Stern and Sunberg, *Trials of Darryl Hunt*, 34:30–34:39.

11. Dr. Eversely estimates that the Committee raised $100,000 over the years.

12. See Sykes Report, 23. Those instances were the cancelling of Hunt's second polygraph, Tisdale's September 12, 1984, interview with Hunt, and the delay of eight months between an identification of Hunt in a photo lineup and the live lineup by Roger Weaver, who had seen Hunt's picture in the paper, before he came forward.

sealed it, and it was never made public, although copies were sent to the DA's Office and the Police Department.[13] Detective Crump said later, "We could not prove Darryl Hunt wasn't involved." Despite his own discovery that Brown's blood type was the same as that in the Sykes rape kit, and despite the many similarities between Regina K.'s wounds and those of Mrs. Sykes, Crump added, "We could not develop anything that led to anyone else being involved."[14]

To many, the Police Department Internal Affairs report was as predictable as it was disappointing. That report concluded that detectives had not manipulated witnesses, that Johnny Gray was paid with informant money not reward money, and that the DA had not taken over the investigation. Finally, the report acknowledged a "few deficiencies" in the investigation, resulting from issues of professionalism. Chief Masten took Daulton's detective shield and suspended two CID supervisors for a brief time. He, in turn, received a letter of reprimand from the City Manager.[15]

The City Manager and Board of Aldermen had, of course, no jurisdiction with regard to the conduct of the District Attorney. Tisdale, as a Democrat, found himself dependent on the votes of African-Americans—a large constituency of the Party in Forsyth County. The Hunt Defense Committee was very active in the 1986 primary election, and Tisdale was defeated. Looking back, Tisdale said that he might not have prosecuted had he known the consequences for his political career. "I cut my own throat prosecuting that case," he said. "I lost 98 percent of the black vote at the last election. I don't think Martin Luther King could have solidified the black vote better than that."[16]

The defense attorneys immediately appealed the verdict on the grounds that the judge improperly allowed Tisdale to read Marie Crawford's recanted statement before the jury and into the record. On May 4, 1989, The North Carolina Supreme Court granted Darryl a new trial in the Sykes case, citing the prejudicial effect of Tisdale's use of Crawford's recanted statement. But he wasn't released from prison—because he was

13. Sykes Report, 27. Superior Court Judge Melzer Morgan released some documents to the defense in 1993.

14. Zerwick, "Murder, Race, Justice," pt. 5.

15. See the Summary of the Stuart Report and the Internal Affairs Report in Sykes Report, 23–24.

16. Zerwick, "Murder, Race, Justice," pt. 4.

serving a different forty-year sentence on yet another charge that stemmed from his relationship to Sammy Mitchell, to which we turn briefly now.

CHARGED AND CONVICTED OF ANOTHER MURDER

In April 1986, Merritt Drayton, a black man, was arrested for his girl-friend's death. Looking for a deal, he told detectives that he had information on an old homicide. He said that at a drink house in 1983 he and two others followed Arthur Wilson outside at 2:00 a.m., robbed him, and beat him to death. He claimed that Darryl and Sammy Mitchell participated in the mugging. Detective Randy Weavil, who had assisted on the Sykes investigation, interviewed people who had been there. Two women, who admitted to having been drunk that night, said they saw Sammy and Darryl there on the evening in question. Another witness said she saw three people attack Wilson. Sammy and Darryl were both indicted. Darryl admitted being at the drink house that night but said he left with a cousin at 11:00 p.m., whereas Sammy had stayed. They were both convicted; Sammy received fifty years and Darryl forty; both appealed and Sammy's appeal was turned down. Many of Darryl's supporters believed that, once again, the police department had framed Darryl with fabricated eyewitness testimony in the absence of material evidence.

However, in November 1989, Darryl's conviction in the Wilson case was overturned.

Euphoria erupted in the streets and homes of Hunt supporters throughout the city. Darryl came home in November on a $50,000 bond raised by the National Council of Churches and secured by a second mortgage on Larry Little's house. Said Hunt,

> It's hard to explain how one really feels after being unjustly convicted and sentenced and put in jail . . . I would like to thank the many people who have supported me with all the many thousands of dollars to the Darryl Hunt Defense Fund . . . and the many letters of concern over the years, which were a great enlightenment and uplifting for me.

Everywhere he went people asked for his autograph and told him they were praying for him. Prompted by reading *The Autobiography of Malcolm X* in prison, Hunt had converted to Islam.

Darryl praying in prison. Credit: © 2003, *Winston-Salem Journal* photo by Ted Richardson

Upon his release, he stayed at the home of Defense Committee leader, Khalid Griggs, a local imam. Some members on the Committee feared that his conversion might cause a problem in the black churches, where much of the money was raised. Reverend Eversley responded, "I don't think that is going to be a problem, because at that point it had become transcendent of faith systems and was a matter of justice."[17] Larry Little signed him up for classes at Winston-Salem State University, and he took a job working in the cafeteria of Reynolds Health Center. Since Little had decided to go to law school, the Defense Committee re-organized. Rev. Mendez became the Chairman and Rev. Eversley its Public Affairs Officer.

A DEAL OFFERED AND REJECTED

District Attorney Don Tisdale's successor, Warren Sparrow, prosecuted Hunt in the first Wilson trial and was set to do the same in the second Sykes trial. However, he cited a conflict of interest in Sykes's case and the N.C. Attorney General appointed a special prosecutor—Dean Bowman of Surry County—for the Sykes re-trial.

In the Wilson case, Sparrow faced newly discovered evidence contradicting Merritt Drayton's claims of Hunt's involvement in the Wilson

17. Panel Discussion in Religion 332: Religion and Public Life, November 8, 2005.

murder. Prosecutor Bowman knew the weaknesses of the evidence against Hunt in the Sykes case, so the two prosecutors came to Hunt with a deal. If he pleaded guilty to lesser charges in both cases, he would be sentenced to time served. If he admitted to killing both Mr. Wilson and Mrs. Sykes, he would not have to go back to prison.

This was an extremely tempting offer. For one thing, his advisors—Mark Rabil, James Ferguson, Larry Little, Rev. Eversley—told him to take the deal. Little said, "Darryl you are not going to get justice in these courts. Even if they had the murder on video tape, they would still convict you. Don't worry, we'll tell people in the community why you had to take the deal." For another, Darryl had already served "hard time" in prison. As a convicted rapist/killer of a white woman, white supremacist gangs in prison regularly threatened his life. They left notes in his cell, saying things like, "Don't turn your head n_____ or you'll be dead." He slept only a few hours a night. He went to the bathroom and took a shower at 3:00 a.m. and had someone watch out for him. He tried never to get soap in his eyes. In one prison, a guard asked him to take some trash to a bin, just outside the grounds, so he could accuse Darryl of trying to escape and shoot him. In another, Darryl heard that some guards had told the "skinheads" that they would bring in dope for them if they killed Darryl.

So the offer was tempting. Rev. Mendez dissented and told Darryl to do what his conscience dictated. Ultimately, Darryl said no. The reasons, he said later, were:

> One, I was innocent. I couldn't see pleading guilty to something that I didn't do. Also, the Sykes family had a mother and daughter who was raped and murdered, so it wouldn't be right for me or for them either. It would be letting [the police] off the hook, because they were supposed to be finding the person who did it.

Although he could have stayed home for good that day, Darryl once again refused to say he had done something he had not done; he fully intended the detectives to have to find Mrs. Sykes's real killer.

Hunt's second trial for the murder of Arthur Wilson went forward in Catawba County in March 1990, and he was acquitted.

RELEASE AND A NEW TRIAL

To handle the defense in the second trial, Little recommended James Ferguson, the well-known civil rights attorney from Charlotte who had successfully overturned the conviction of the Wilmington Ten, back in the 1970s. Ferguson made motions to move the Wilson and Sykes re-trial away from Forsyth County to an urban county with a similar racial profile. The judges agreed but could not find space on the calendar in any of those counties. The trial took place in Newton, also in Catawba County. Two predominantly white Christian groups filed *amicus curiae* briefs supporting Hunt—the Presbyterian Synod of the Piedmont and the Forsyth Ministerial Association.[18] In the second Sykes trial, Winston-Salem detectives came to special prosecutor Bowman's aid. Assigned to the re-investigation were Randy Weavil—lead detective for the Wilson case and assistant in the first Sykes investigation—and Teresa Hicks—lead in the Linda E. and Kathleen D. cases and assistant in the Sykes case. To add to Gray, Murphy, and Crawford, the detectives came up with three new witnesses implicating Hunt, and Bowman decided to go forward with a second trial.

Kevey Coleman, the first of these three new witnesses, came to the attention of the police department in May 1986, during the SBI investigation. A co-worker called in a tip and said that Coleman should be interviewed. In 1984, Coleman worked the night shift at the Coke bottling plant and lived near the site of Deborah Sykes's murder. On August 10, a friend dropped him off and, as he walked home, he saw two black men with a white woman on the corner. In an interview with an SBI agent and Detectives Carter Crump and Riley Spoon, Coleman later claimed that he first identified Willard Brown as one of the men he saw. The official report said simply that he saw two black men but could not identify them because he wasn't wearing his contact lenses.[19] Between 1986 and the beginning of the second trial in September 1990, Coleman was interviewed five more times. He claims that he felt that, because he was black and admitted to having been in the vicinity of the murder, the SBI agents and WSPD detectives treated him as a suspect. In each of his successive statements, he was increasingly willing to say that the two men may have looked like Darryl Hunt and Sammy Mitchell.

18. Eversley, Interview, 2010. Reverend L.V. Lassiter of the Grace Presbyterian Church led the effort in the Synod, renamed the Synod of the Mid-Atlantic. Reverend Hank Keating, Associate Pastor of the First Presbyterian Church, served as President of the Ministerial Alliance.

19. The interview was not taped, and this identification was not documented in the SBI file. Coleman made this claim in a 2005 interview with the Sykes Review Committee investigators. WSPD Detective Spoon said he does not recall Willard Brown's name being mentioned in this May 1986 interview. See Sykes Report, 60–61.

In the 1989 re-investigation, Coleman signed a statement stating, "I have seen the photographs of Darryl Hunt and Sammy Mitchell. I'm not 100 percent sure, but I would honestly say that they are the two people I saw with her."[20] But by the second trial, Coleman seemed sure, "I see someone who looks like one of the persons I saw—Mr. Hunt, over there."[21] However, in a later statement, he said that he was prepared to testify that he had first identified Willard Brown as the person in question.[22] Unfortunately, Jim Ferguson, Hunt's attorney, did not have Coleman's SBI statement until the day he testified. After the trial, Ferguson obtained the statement of Coleman's wife that he couldn't identify anyone the day of the murder and that detectives had offered him reward money for his testimony after they had threatened him with arrest. He had no idea that Coleman may have initially identified Brown, as that was not a part of the official report.

The second new witness—a woman—came forward saying that she had seen Hunt and Mitchell in the vicinity of the crime scene on the morning of the murder. The defense pointed out that she was on probation for welfare fraud and wanted "to gain favor with the police."[23] Ed Reese, the third new witness and father of one of Sammy Mitchell's siblings, testified that he had seen Mitchell alone that morning. It was later learned that Reese suffered from dementia.[24] On the basis of these two testimonies, Sammy Mitchell was indicted for Mrs. Sykes's murder.[25]

By 1990, Thomas Murphy testified that, instead of two men, there were four black men with Mrs. Sykes. Johnny Gray, serving a fifty-three-year sentence for murdering a man in 1988, pretty much stuck to his story. Marie Crawford, though, changed hers yet again, testifying that only Hunt had spent the night with her on August 9, 1984, that he was gone when she got up but returned later with blood on his hand, not grass stains on his pants. She said that he later confessed to her that he and Mitchell both robbed Mrs. Sykes, but that Sammy was the one who killed her.[26]

20. Zewick, "Murder, Race, Justice," pt. 5.

21. Ibid., pt. 4.

22. See Sykes Report, 58–61.

23. Zerwick, "Murder, Race, Justice," pt. 6.

24. Mark Rabil, interview by author, May 11, 2009.

25. Despite the indictment, no Forsyth County District Attorney ever tried Mitchell for Mrs. Sykes's murder.

26. Zerwick, "Murder, Race, Justice," pt. 5.

Johnny Gray accuses Darryl at second trial. Credit: © 1990
Winston-Salem Journal photo by Allen Aycock

For good measure, into this mix the state threw a jailhouse "snitch." In
a letter to the District Attorney, Jessie Moore, serving time for armed robbery, said that he knew Hunt was guilty and used the term "White Rose" of
Mrs. Sykes—a Klan term for a white Christian woman. At trial he testified
that he had heard Hunt say, "That was pretty good stuff; he'd like to do it all
over again." In exchange for his testimony, Moore received parole.[27]

The defense aimed to raise reasonable doubts about the testimonies
of all the witnesses.

Hunt and Rabil during the second trial. © 1990
Winston-Salem Journal photo by Allen Aycock

27. Stern and Sunberg, *Trials of Darryl Hunt*, 43.51.

For example, Ferguson confronted Johnny Gray, who was by this time serving a life sentence for murder.[28]

"You told the police that your name was Sammy Mitchell."

"That's what *they* say."

"Do you deny to this jury now that the name you gave that morning was Sammy Mitchell?"

"If the tape says I said the name Sammy Mitchell, it's possible I did say that. I'm not denying anything."

"You knew who Sammy Mitchell was, didn't you?"

"I didn't know no Sammy Mitchell."

"Didn't you tell a police officer that you had seen Sammy Mitchell at least a thousand times before August 10, 1984?"

"I don't know what officer told you that, but if he told you that, he lied."

"So, you just pulled the name of Sammy Mitchell out of the blue sky."

"If you want the answer to that, you've got to turn to Jesus, because I can't answer that."

Then, Ferguson read the statements of his old poolroom buddy, Al Kelly, who said during the SBI investigation that Gray admitted both raping and robbing Mrs. Sykes. Gray denied Kelly's assertions one by one.[29]

In his closing, Ferguson appealed to the jurors' reason, asking them to look at the credibility of each witness:

> What I have heard from the prosecution is a case of extraordinarily low quality, and the state has tried to make up in quantity what it lacks in quality. But I have to say to you that a pile of trash does not get better as it gets bigger. It simply makes it more difficult to sift through to see if there's anything of value.[30]

He surveyed the witnesses and lack of material evidence and kept returning to the trash pile refrain. It was a virtuoso performance in the style of African-American preaching, and yet Rev. Mendez said, "I never felt like they heard him."

Dean Bowman saw the weaknesses of the case as a challenge.

---

28. Sykes Report, 69. Gray was convicted in 1988 for the beating death of Willis Mabe during a robbery.

29. Zerwick, "Murder, Race, Justice," pt. 6.

30. Ibid.

The most fulfilling thing about being a prosecutor is that . . . you know you are doing the right thing . . . You have a moral conviction that truth will come out. You just have to trudge on, no matter what the odds are against you . . . And in doing that, you become very passionate about that . . . If you believe that to be the truth, then it will prevail. And I've found that it does.[31]

Though Bowman did have a weak case to argue, he had other advantages. He took full advantage of the state's weak discovery laws by waiting until the day a witness testified to give Ferguson a copy of the statement. To a request for DNA testing of the semen sample in the rape kit, Bowman responded—inaccurately, as it turned out—that the sample was too degraded for a test.[32] In addition, the judge denied Ferguson's discovery motion for access to the 1986 SBI report.

In his closing argument, Bowman went not for the head, but for the gut.

Dean Bowman makes his closing argument. Credit: ©1990 Winston-Salem Journal photo by Stephen Matteson, Jr.

He laid out Deborah Sykes's bloody clothes and pictures of her taken at the scene in front of the jury:

"She put on this light blouse here when she got up to go to work," he said, holding up the sleeveless knit blouse caked with mud and blood.

31. Stern and Sunberg, *Trials of Darryl Hunt*, 48:39.
32. See below.

"Maybe she was thinking of having a baby," he said, as some of the jurors began to cry.[33]

"And what was she thinking when this man right over here, this Darryl Eugene Hunt, what was she thinking when he pinned her down to the ground, held her arms up and he slashed her and he slashed her and he slashed her and he slashed her some more, just like he was butchering some animal?

"Finally, what was Deborah Sykes thinking—this real person Deborah Sykes—when this man right over here—what was she thinking when he spread those legs right there apart and he crawled down inside her and he raped and ravaged her and deposited some thick yellow sickening fluid in her body? Did she feel the blood trickling down her back and neck? Did she feel the blood running down her legs? Did she feel the life trickle out of her body, right there on the grass?

"What hope did Deborah Sykes cling to then? Where was the judge and where was the jury? When life's blood ran on the grass?"

Then, pointing at Darryl, Bowman ranted to the jury: "He's a robber and rapist and a kidnapper and a sadistic butcher."

Bowman's theatrics worked for some in the room. Mary Anne Sheboy, the reporter for the Winston-Salem television station, WXII, recounted,

> I had tears coming down my face, because I felt that I was Deborah Sykes that morning. And when he was done, I was just as convinced that Hunt was guilty as I was after the first trial.

It must have worked for some of the jurors, too. In less than two hours, they convicted Hunt of first-degree murder in the course of committing four felonies—robbery, kidnapping, sexual assault, and rape. In the initial pool of one hundred potential jurors, four had been black; none of those made it onto what turned out to be an all-white panel.

After sentencing him, again, to life in prison, the judge asked Darryl if he had something to say. Darryl replied shaking his head, "I am innocent of these charges, even though I have been found guilty."[34]

So on October 12, 1990, Darryl went back to prison. For him, his supporters, and many others in Winston-Salem, anger and frustration replaced the euphoria of his release eleven months earlier. Little, referring to the snitch Jesse Moore's performance, was exasperated:

33. Zerwick, "Murder, Race, Justice," pt. 6.

34. Stern and Sunberg, *Trials of Darryl Hunt*, 48:22.

> It's just incredible what's gong on. And what does the media do? The media basically—not all of them—but most of them turns a blind eye, or winks at this b.s. that is going on. White people to this day don't realize that this sort of stuff was going on, because the mainstream white reporters did not cover it like this.[35]

Ferguson commented later:

> It's difficult to describe the feeling that you get when you realize that, in spite of your very best efforts to get justice, that you can't get it. And it makes you wonder, for a moment, is there really any hope at all.[36]

Behind and underneath all of these events, Larry Little saw the ugly, irrational head of racism:

> You could have been F. Lee Bailey, Johnny Cochran, Jim Ferguson; racism is more powerful than facts. Because racism is illogical and it is emotional and, therefore, facts don't matter.[37]

Due to the work of the CID of the Winston-Salem Police Department and two prosecutors, what had been very fragile evidence against Hunt in the fall of 1984 now looked much more substantial. The verdict of the second jury cemented Hunt's guilt in the minds of many in the Winston-Salem community and in the judicial system, as we will see. However, a few members of the Hunt Defense Committee and Mark Rabil refused to give up and kept working together to free Darryl.

APPEALS FALL ON DEAF EARS

Mark Rabil believed that, in order to free Darryl, the defense team would have to solve the crime. So they hired yet another investigator who found other eyewitnesses who had been ignored or intimidated by the police and prosecutors in the first and second trials. One stated, in a deposition, "They [the police] got talkin' to me. You ain't goin' downtown now to testify are you? You know that damned nigger is guilty."

The defense team, through a new appellate attorney, Ben Dowling-Sendor, filed an appeal, citing witness intimidation and the suppression of exculpatory evidence on the part of the prosecution. Several witnesses

35. Ibid.
36. Ibid., 48:55.
37. Ibid., 50:00.

testified that Johnny Gray had confessed to lying about Darryl and had, himself, participated in the murder of Mrs. Sykes. Gray's former girl-friend, Lisa McBride, stated that he had once stabbed her in the shoulder and said that he would kill her as he had Mrs. Sykes. Sendor pressed Superior Court Judge Melzer Morgan for the SBI report and documents. When Morgan refused, Dowling-Sendor appealed to the North Carolina Supreme Court who released much of the three thousand-page report. The defense discovered that much of this material should have been given to them before the second trial under the landmark Brady v. Maryland decision on the handing over of exculpatory evidence. Among the revelations were that Bowman had suppressed eight of the thirteen statements Kevey Coleman had made to the police.

More important, there was a series of reports in the SBI files that showed that the state knew that DNA testing was possible prior to the second trial in 1990, that the prosecutors could have tested to find out who had assaulted Deborah, but just as Detective Crump had decided not to do the voice recognition lineup on Willard Brown in 1986, so the state prosecutors decided not to do a DNA test on the semen in the rape kit.

The defense team made a motion to do a DNA test. The new District Attorney in Forsyth County, Tom Keith, strenuously objected.[38] Eric Saunders, his assistant, supported his objection with a curious argument:

> I would submit to you that what this court knows about DNA testing is that it is a highly speculative procedure. And I would submit to you that neither side would be happy with the results.[39]

This is curious because the defense had asked for the test. Throughout the process, Darryl had wanted the DNA test to be done. It was the state that seemed to fear the results.

Hedging his bets, the DA's assistant Saunders continued,

> The state's contention is that this crime was committed by two people. Sammy Mitchell could have been raping and abusing Mrs. Sykes while Darryl Hunt was providing a lookout and going through her pocketbook.[40]

---

38. Keith, a Republican, defeated Sparrow in the 1990 election.

39. Stern and Sunberg, *Trials of Darryl Hunt*, 54:42.

40. Ibid., 55:08.

Ferguson countered that the state had been unequivocal that Darryl had been the one on top of Mrs. Sykes and commented quizzically to the judge, "So now they are saying they didn't really mean that?"

Judge Morgan denied the claim of witness intimidation and ruled that the withheld evidence was not sufficiently important to warrant a new trial. However, he did grant the motion for the DNA testing. Again, hopes were high that the exposure of the misconduct of the police investigators and prosecutors in the first two trials would finally free Darryl and he would go home for good.

The results were stunning. On October 22, 1993, a forensic scientist phoned Mark Rabil and told him that the DNA material results excluded both Darryl and Sammy Mitchell. Rabil, again, was ecstatic:

> I have to say that was one of the happiest seconds in my life and my legal career. At that moment I had absolutely no doubt that that was the end of the case.

He believed that finally there was irrefutable physical evidence proving Darryl's innocence. Darryl and his supporters knew that this time his fate was beyond the reach of the racial prejudice and the recalcitrance of police and prosecutors. Finally, he would be coming home. Rabil went to talk to Darryl at the prison.

"What are you going to do when you get out of here?"

Darryl replied, "I have to give back or try to give back some of [what] the people have given me in these last ten years. So, I think, in my heart, I have to give back to the community—and hope that the travesty that happened to me for these last ten years doesn't happen to someone else."[41]

In November 1994, Hunt packed his pictures and books, gave away other personal items to other inmates, and prepared to come home.

Dowling-Sendor filed a Motion for Appropriate Relief asking for the release of Hunt:

> I'll be filing a motion to the state Supreme Court today so that Darryl Hunt can finally see justice and freedom and so that the state can get on with the business of finding the real rapist and real killer of Deborah Sykes and so this community might actually begin to heal after this ordeal.[42]

41. Ibid., 58:49.
42. Ibid., 59:37.

The state had persistently argued that Hunt or Mitchell had to have been present at the crime scene. Therefore, Assistant DA, Eric Saunders, reaching for straws, argued that the results were inconceivable and that there must have been some sort of contamination.

A juror in the first trial, upon hearing that Darryl Hunt's DNA was not found on Mrs. Sykes's body, said, "Sounds like he may be innocent and if he is, thank the Lord we didn't put him to death."[43]

Judge Morgan, in a ruling as stunning as the DNA results, stated that the results proved only that while Hunt could have raped the victim he may not have ejaculated. Other creative theories offered by the district attorney, the judge, and a NC Supreme Court Justice included: Hunt may have held her while someone else murdered her, or he may have raped and murdered her, but someone came along after her death and raped her, masking Hunt's semen. While judges all over the country had dismissed charges against defendants on the basis of newly refined DNA testing technology, this judge denied the appeal and the request for a new trial.

Asked by a reporter whether the DNA test meant that Winston-Salem should be frightened, knowing the true murderer is still out there haunting the streets, Saunders replied, "Well, I believe that is a little exaggerated." In fact, Willard Brown was indeed on the streets of Winston-Salem as Saunders spoke.[44] Neither the district attorney's office nor the police department ever reopened the investigation to find the source of the DNA, though it seems that Detective Crump and, perhaps, several others in the Police Department might have made it a short investigation.

The legal defense team and the Defense Committee were devastated. As Morgan read his ruling, Rev. Mendez stood and said, "This is an evil, ungodly, corrupt court." The bailiff asked him to leave the courtroom. Larry Little observed bitterly, "That is the nature of racism. That is the arrogance of power. Their motto is 'If the shoe doesn't fit, then break the foot and put the shoe on.'" Rev. Eversley wept at the press conference and condemned the judgment calling it "cracker justice." Mendez kicked Eversley under the table, to warn him not to antagonize the white community. Eversley responded,

> John, stop kicking me, I know exactly what I'm saying and why I'm saying it. It wasn't to offend white people, it was to say that cracker

43. Zerwick, "Murder, Race, Justice," pt. 6.

44. Sykes Report, Appendix 5, June 1984 Willard Brown Prison Release Documents.

justice is justice that looks at the evidence and says, "Damn the evidence, hang the nigger."[45]

Jim Ferguson read a statement from Darryl to the press:

> I pray that I, too, can turn this injustice into something meaningful for my brothers, sisters, and community as a whole. I pray above all else that you all will keep in mind and prayers the many, many other Darryl Hunts on which racism and injustice has rained. And without you many will not have the strength or the courage to overcome the atrocities inflicted upon them.[46]

Appellate attorney Ben Dowling-Sendor called the decision a "judicial lynching":

> Darryl Hunt has not been physically lynched, but he's been judicially lynched on evidence that any reasonable person would conclude does not only not convict Darryl Hunt, but proves his innocence. . . . I sure hope that the Supreme Court of North Carolina will show that, in fact, most of North Carolina is in the twentieth century for good.

Unfortunately, that did not happen. The defense appealed Judge Morgan's ruling to the North Carolina Supreme Court. On December 30, 1994, Mark Rabil made a heart-breaking call to Darryl Hunt, "I'm sorry, Darryl, we lost four-to-three." By that vote, the Court had turned down the appeal. Darryl listened on the hall phone at the Rowan Correctional Facility in Salisbury, North Carolina. Larry Little and Carlton Eversley were in Rabil's office that day. In tears, Little assured Darryl that they would immediately file an appeal with the U.S. Supreme Court: "We'll take this thing national. Everyone needs to know about what happened to you." Facing the rest of his life in prison, Darryl said, "Thank everyone for me." Then, a dial tone punctured the silence.[47] Darryl said later that, as painful as it was for him to be turned down again, "this had been happening to me all the time, so I'd done got kind of immune to being discarded."[48]

45. Panel Discussion, REL 320: Religion and Public Life, November 9, 2005.

46. Stern and Sunberg, *Trials of Darryl Hunt*, 108:09.

47. Stern and Sundberg captured this poignant scene. See *Trials of Darryl Hunt*, 1:11:00ff.

48. Ibid., 1:09:36.

HOPE DIES

Rabil filed a habeas corpus petition in the Fourth Federal District Court. One hundred supporters traveled to Richmond on buses, including two busloads of students from Winston-Salem State University. Rabil argued that the DNA exclusion refuted the state's theory of the case and that the prosecutors in the second trial failed to turn over three thousand pages of evidence that contradicted the eyewitness testimony putting Darryl at the scene. The Court rejected the petition, as did the Fourth U.S. Court of Appeals in February 2000. Rabil appealed to the U.S. Supreme Court in June. On October 16, 2000, he learned that the U.S. Supreme Court refused to hear the case. Of the fifty cases in the country in which DNA had excluded people in rape and murder cases, this was the only case in which the Court rejected that evidence. It was the end of the road.

Larry Little, incensed by the 1985 verdict, had gone to Wake Forest Law School and had graduated at the top of his class. On learning of this Supreme Court decision, he gave up the practice of law, completely disillusioned with the criminal justice system. He now teaches political science at Winston-Salem State University. Jim Ferguson saw the decision as "the gravest of injustices, that would probably go uncorrected. And Darryl Hunt would spend his life in jail for a crime that he did not commit."[49] Mark Rabil turned his attention to his wife, who was dying of cancer. John Mendez experienced such a crisis of faith that he considered leaving the ministry. And Winston-Salem remained deeply divided over the case.

Since Darryl's arrest, there had been—among his supporters—repeated cycles of shock, anger, and frustration, followed by glimmers of hope, euphoria, and celebration. Now, the last door had been slammed shut.

It seemed as if the police department and the district attorney's office were committed to defending the investigations and convictions, twisting the evidence into ever more fantastical theories, and refusing to investigate leads that didn't fit them. Once the evidence—such as it was—made it before juries and those juries rendered verdicts, the judicial review process—that tends to respect those verdicts—seemed paralyzed. Judges at every level joined the state in generating possible scenarios to explain why the DNA exclusion should not warrant a new trial.[50] It got to

49. Ibid., 1:17:29ff.

50. See Rabil's "Petition for Commutation," 11–13 for the evolving theories of the state and the various levels of the judicial review.

the point that the defense would have had to prove all possible theories of the evidence wrong before relief would be granted.

Possible relief from a political process was not likely either. The City Council had commissioned the 1986 City Manager's report. There was one demotion, a couple of suspensions, and the reprimand of the Chief. With respect to the District Attorney's Office and the judicial process, the Council saw itself as impotent.

The mainstream media, particularly the daily *Winston-Salem Journal*, covered the fourteen-year saga by simply reporting the competing claims of the state and the Defense Committee, without investigating or evaluating their merit. In addition, by characterizing the leaders of the Hunt Defense Committee as, for example, "black activists," pastors, or the "former Black Panther, Larry Little," the *Journal* contributed to the racially polarized context of the events. The result was that many of the city's white population assumed that Little, Mendez, Eversley, and Griggs were defending Darryl simply because he was black. Further, a number felt that, even if he hadn't committed this crime, he was probably guilty of something.

There seemed to be no stone left unturned. Darryl and those who had fought for him so courageously, persistently, and sacrificially had met defeat. For many, anger and frustration finally gave way to despair and resignation. There was no way out.

Meanwhile, I'm guessing that the majority of whites, like me to that point, had not paid a lot of attention to any of this.

three

It's *My* Business?

In late June 1985, I moved to Winston-Salem to begin a teaching position in the Religion Department at Wake Forest University. Born in Bluefield, West Virginia, I grew up in Bristol, Tennessee, received a bachelor's degree from the University of Tennessee and then a master's and a doctoral degree from Harvard Divinity School.

From my arrival in Winston-Salem through Darryl Hunt's second trial and the various appeals processes that lasted until Spring 2003, I do not recall reading or watching any of the stories about the case in the news media. I don't remember any friend or colleague at Wake Forest mentioning it. In the 1980s, I did not subscribe to the daily newspaper—*The Winston-Salem Journal*—that served a predominantly white constituency, or to the black-owned, weekly paper, *The Winston-Salem Chronicle*. I occasionally read the *Journal*, but did not become aware of the *Chronicle's* existence until later. Periodically, I would watch the local television news shows. But frankly I paid absolutely no attention to what I now know was the generous and sensational media coverage of the on-going saga.

Why is that? Well, it just didn't seem like it was much of my business.

For the most part, my attention was absorbed by the professional responsibilities involved in making a successful application for tenure and by the personal issues that led to my divorce.

FAITHFULLY MINDING MY OWN BUSINESS

Things went fairly well on the first front. I revised and published my dissertation with a university press, as well as a number of articles on sixteenth-century Anabaptists.

My doctoral work was on the history of Christianity in Europe, and my dissertation focused on a Reformation figure, Pilgram Marpeck—a forerunner of the Mennonite, Hutterite, and Amish traditions. The groups Marpeck related to were pacifist—a stance I found appealing. They believed that no one should be forced by the state to believe, or say that they believe, anything and that a Christian should not engage in any form of physical violence, particularly deadly force (using a sword, in their context), against even the worst offenders. For them, when Jesus told his followers to "turn the other cheek," he meant it. Most refused to take vows that committed them to carry a weapon in order to protect the cities they lived in; some even refused to pay taxes that might be used to support military purposes.

Having lived through the Vietnam era, I respected their belief that violence is not always the best way to resolve disputes. I wondered, however, whether their sectarian withdrawal and absolute commitment to non-resistance was sufficient to assure justice in the world. I was attracted to Marpeck because he expressed concern not only for righteousness in relation to God but also justice in relation to his fellow human beings. He did not reject the oath of loyalty to the cities he lived in and the commitment it entailed to their defense. He objected, however, to state violence that too often protected the interests of a privileged few at a cost paid by those who could not avoid military service. Rather than withdraw from those civic communities—as many other Anabaptists did—he engaged in professional activities as a municipal engineer, providing water and firewood to his fellow citizens. He affirmed the positive role the state played in providing for the common good while resisting its intrusion into matters of religious faith and practice. Rather than non-resistance, Marpeck's approach can better be described as non-violent resistance.

When I began teaching at Wake Forest, I ascribed, I suppose, to a "color-blind" posture on race. I believed it to be unjust that one's race or color would limit one's educational, political, or economic opportunities. However, implicitly I guess I thought that agitating for more of those opportunities was the responsibility, or business, of those most affected—African American people themselves.

Shortly after my arrival at Wake Forest, conversations with black students and the few African-American professors on the faculty convinced me that I should do more to level the playing field. They argued that the success of black students depends, in part, on having more black professors to model the possibilities open to them. Consequently, a few years after arriving at Wake Forest, I joined others in the Religion Department in advocating for the hiring of an African-American colleague, Alton Pollard, who taught sociology of religion and whom I had met at Harvard.

Things did not go so well on the other, personal front. My wife and I separated in 1986 and divorced in 1987. In the midst of that process, I discovered a new area of academic research and therapeutic practice—men's studies and men's work. These helped me not only to understand my part in the dynamics leading to the divorce, but also to develop new, healthier ways of thinking, feeling, and acting.

Men's studies, or the critical study of men and masculinities, explore men's socialization and conditioning not simply as an outgrowth of our male biology but as socially created and culturally specific expectations. These expectations can be helpful and productive or they can be counterproductive for men's health and relationships. I learned that some masculine expectations cause tensions in our lives. For example, men are not supposed to express our emotions freely; if we do, we can be targeted with ridicule, humiliation, and even violence. Suppressing our emotions can encourage us not to allow them into our consciousness to begin with. That, in turn, often adversely affects our health and our relationships with others, including those with whom we are most intimate. We are also taught to be competitive—to outdistance other men in the measures of manhood. Early in life, this often takes the form of athletic prowess and later, in financial and career success. If we have managerial responsibilities at work, competitiveness and the resentment it routinely produces in those around us can undermine the cooperation our jobs require for success. In other words, there are inherent conflicts between some of the expectations we believe we must fulfill to gain respect as men.[1]

In the early 1990s, a "men's movement" grew among predominantly white, middle-class professionals. Led by the likes of Robert Bly, Michael Meade, and Sam Keen, many of these men turned to Native-

---

1. Social psychologist Joseph Pleck has developed a sex-role strain theory to explain some of the ways that masculine conditioning can be dysfunctional for men. See Peck, "Gender Role Strain Paradigm."

American traditions, rituals, and perspectives for inspiration and healing. Drumming circles, sharing from the heart with the use of a "talking
stick," smudging with burnt sage, sweat lodges, and "new warrior" week-
ends became common practices for many men. I attended several of
these retreats and found them helpful in getting leverage on some of the
masculine expectations I found counterproductive. I wrote a book about
what I learned both academically and practically, helped start scholarly
groups in my field, and led a number of retreats for men.[2]

A WAKE-UP CALL

In the midst of this work, I gave a presentation in a department collo-
quium about the aspect of the men's movement that encouraged mostly
white men like me to go into the woods, literally or figuratively outside
the heavy responsibilities of our institutional duties, where we could find
"sacred space" to heal and to choose, more intentionally, the ways we
wanted to live.[3] My aforementioned new African-American colleague,
Alton Pollard, said, "Steve, you don't have to go out in the woods for
that. All you have to do is drive over to East Winston [the predominantly
African-American part of our town]."[4] I had heard about a local, bi-racial
organization—Citizens United for Justice—that met at Emmanuel Baptist
Church and was led by the pastor, Reverend John Mendez.

A week later, as I drove toward the church, I had a number of anxious
thoughts running through my head: "What will they think—a white guy
showing up to their meeting? What will they say? Will they say anything
to me? I wonder if it is a dangerous part of town? Will the church parking
lot be safe? Why am I doing this?" My heart was pounding; I was short
of breath; my knuckles turned white as I gripped the steering wheel. "I'll
turn around. I'll go next week," I assuaged myself. "But wait a minute, I
can't not go; Alton is a colleague and friend; he goes to his church every
week. Can't I even go over there one time?" I kept driving. "I'll go this one

---

2. See Boyd, *Men We Long to Be*. Two colleagues and I collected and published papers
given at the Men's Studies in Religion Group of the American Academy of Religion. See
Boyd, Mark Muesse, and Merle Longwood, *Redeeming Men*, and my contribution, "Mas-
culinity and Male Dominance: Martin Luther and the Punishment of Adam" (19–32).

3. The next two paragraphs first appeared in Culbertson, "Spirituality of Men," 48–49.

4. Dr. Pollard left Wake Forest to direct the Black Church Studies Program at Emory
University and now serves as Dean of the Howard University Divinity School.

time. How bad can it be? If they don't like me, I'll just slip out and that will be that; I will have tried."

When I arrived, it didn't take me long to realize that the source of my anxiety was completely in my own head. The group welcomed me warmly, asked why I had come, and then went on with the business of the evening. Starting that night, I heard person after person (mostly working-class black, but also some white people) come and talk about what had happened to them in our city's courts, police station, schools, and businesses. What I heard changed my life. There was a rich world of people, relationships, institutions, and history about which I knew next to nothing. I couldn't believe that all of this had been virtually invisible to me. Though we lived in the same town, we did not live in the same place.[5]

AN ELEPHANT IN THE CITY

That evening and over the next several years I learned a number of important things. I realized that those who came to these meetings were more like me than not. They, like me, wanted opportunities for a good education and meaningful work. They wanted freedom from violence, health care, and good, life-giving relationships with others, including me.

It also became clear that their lives were affected by racial and class dynamics in ways mine was not. For example, I heard stories from middle-class and professional black men who had been pulled over by policemen for no apparent reason—other than that they were black. I learned, too, that following a judge's desegregation order in 1971 and a period of busing, the city/county schools were moving again toward racial segregation, due to a "neighborhood school" assignment plan adopted by the predominantly white school board in 1993. In our schools, expulsions and suspensions are meted out to African-American students—males in particular—at a rate disproportionate to their numbers in the school system. For some young, African-American males, these suspensions and expulsions contributed to their falling behind in their schoolwork and became a precursor to incarceration. I saw how that happened in the life of Frank, a black teenager I met.

At the invitation of a member of Citizens United for Justice, I started attending events at the Winston-Salem Urban League. Among those was a three-day workshop called "Bridging the Gaps in Race Relations." A

5. See Fulkerson, *Places of Redemption*.

group composed of an equal number of whites and blacks gathered for instruction about African-American history and culture and for structured dialogue about issues that emerged in the course of the workshop.

At fifteen, Frank had already been arrested several times for drug dealing and had recently been released from a juvenile detention center. The Urban League staff got him involved in several programs, including this one, to try to offer alternatives to his life on the street with the hope of keeping him from a life of crime and the prospect of spending much of it in jail. At one point, he told a little of his story. He lived with his mom, who worked and was gone a lot. When he was around twelve and wanted the basketball shoes and jewelry that some guys in the neighborhood had, he began delivering drugs for the dealers. Then, he began selling them himself. The money he made was considerable—hundreds of dollars in one deal, thousands over the course of a month.

Another of the participants was a black man in his early-thirties named Henry who was involved in real estate and development. He drove a very impressive late-model sports car and dressed immaculately. When our group sessions first began, I thought, "Oh, I see. Frank can hear about Henry and learn how to get what he wants another way." But then, Henry told his story. He was a college graduate and had been involved in real estate for a while. He talked in detail about how frustrating it was for him to get turned down by banks and lending institutions for loans to purchase new properties when he knew other (white) developers no more qualified then he who were getting loans approved. His frustration bordered on bitterness as he talked about getting out of that line of business and doing something else.

So I could imagine that young Frank may have seen his options this way: "I can stay in school, where there are some teachers that seem either scared of me, indifferent to whether I learn anything, or oblivious to the way my life is. I can work a job at McDonald's at minimum wage and, if I work really hard for a long time and get some breaks, I can go to college and someday do what Henry is doing and face even more obstacles. Or I can buy and sell drugs, make as much or more money than Henry is making, and have what I want and take care of my mother—right now." I could see how risking another stint in juvenile detention or later in prison might seem worth it.

It wasn't clear to me at the time how much of the discrimination Henry felt was real and how much was imagined. But since that time I have learned that there is, in plenty of communities, collusion between realtors and lending institutions in an unofficial and unacknowledged policy of "red-lining" that feeds residential, racial segregation. There are also informal networks of public utilities board members and officers in financial institutions—networks that include white builders and developers in the division of the economic pie and that exclude others. These practices are illegal, but because of the nature of the informal relationships in which they take place, it is very difficult to gather the evidence necessary to challenge them in court.

What was clear to me was that Henry believed that he was the target of such discrimination and exclusion *because he was black*. I imagine that Frank believed it too. And that belief shaped what he believed to be possible for him in his life as a whole.

What was also clear to me was that as a black male, even if you kept your nose clean, stayed in school, and got a job, you might still wind up in jail, through no fault of you own.

A FRIEND FALSELY CHARGED

In the mid-1990s, I developed a relationship with a twenty-five-year-old African-American man, Geoffrey Fulton. We coached the church league basketball team that represented our predominantly white and black churches, which partnered in joint projects. His parents were middle-class professionals, active in their local church and in civic affairs. One night at about 8:00 p.m. six police cars came to their house with sirens screaming and lights blazing. They came to question my friend about a string of jewelry store robberies in four counties. He was not home, but his parents were made to sit on the couch while their house was searched. Though no material evidence was ever found relating him to any of the robberies, my friend was arrested and charged with all of them. He had nothing to do with any of them. In fact, he was on the clock at his job in Winston-Salem forty miles away when one of the robberies took place. However, on the basis of a picture lineup, he was identified by two white women as having participated in one of the incidents, and by another white woman in a second robbery. Due to flimsy evidence, a magistrate in a third county dismissed the charges.

Attending the trials and hearings, I discovered that the detectives— all white—in each of the counties had worked together simply because each of the robberies allegedly had been committed by an African-American male.

My friend came under suspicion when he and two female friends entered a store in a neighboring county and asked to look at a particular watch. Earlier in the week a detective had been in the store and had showed the clerk a composite sketch of the robber—a young African-American male. When my friend asked to see the watch, the clerk went to the back and called security, because he thought my friend resembled the sketch. Security followed my friend out of the store and took his license number. That led to the convergence on his home the following week. In the meantime, his picture was included in a picture lineup and shown to two female customers who had witnessed the robbery in that store, as well as to another white female witness of a robbery in another county. The perpetrator in each case was said to be a relatively dark-skinned African-American male. The pictures included in the lineups shown to the women were of five relatively light skinned black males . . . and my friend, who is a dark-skinned black male. In each case they understandably pointed to my friend's picture. I say understandably because what I have since learned is that peoples' tendencies in picture or live lineups is to identify the person or image that looks *most like* the person they saw. While attending a hearing for one of these robberies, a witness from a fourth county was brought to the courtroom door and asked if she saw anyone in the courtroom who looked like the person she had witnessed robbing the store. She picked out my dark-skinned friend, sitting at the defense table. He was then charged in that county. He ended up standing trial in three counties.

In the first trial, even though the defense lawyer for my friend had the time card showing that he was at work forty miles away during the time of the robbery, the District Attorney went forward with his two white female witnesses. After the jury was impaneled, the judge asked the DA for his opening statement. As he did, the two white women—who had been looking over at my friend at the defense table—tugged on the sleeve of the DA and began whispering to him. The DA asked to approach the bench, and the judge announced a recess—before opening statements— and the two attorneys retired with him to his chambers. Fifteen minutes later the judge returned and announced that the charges were dismissed. The defense attorney told us that the two women, seeing my friend for the first time in person, could not be sure about their identification and, since the prosecution's case depended completely on their testimony, the DA decided not to go forward. My friend was not so fortunate in the second and third trials, as the three witnesses in those trials stuck to their identifications. In one of the counties, another witness had identified another African-American male she saw leaving the store and driving away in a car that was traced by police to a younger man with several juvenile violations on his record. However, that lead was never fully investigated after another witness picked out my friend from the picture lineup. The white judge summarily denied every defense motion, including the prejudicial character of the lineup and, moreover, I overheard him ask the bailiff—during a break—if he thought the defense would appeal his rulings. So my friend was convicted, given probation, and fined several thousand dollars. In the third trial, he was convicted and served twenty-eight days in the county jail. Though I'll never be certain, it appeared that the detectives had decided to close five cases with one "suspect," had created three eyewitness identifications with dubious procedures, and had shored up their witnesses after the charges were dropped in the first trial.

This whole episode was very upsetting—primarily to my friend and his family, but also to me and several white friends who attended the trials. We didn't think such shabby police work and prejudicial judicial treatment were possible. We learned that they are not only possible but that many African-Americans actually expect nothing more. I'll never forget a comment by my friend's father in a parking lot some time after my friend's release. When I expressed regret for the considerable money he had had to spend to defend his son from these spurious charges, he replied, "It's only a year of college tuition." I remember thinking, "Do we live in a country in which white people put money in a college fund for their children, while African-American parents of a son have to put money into a defense fund, in case he is ever caught in one of these criminal justice nets?"

Part of what was upsetting was that I and other white friends who became involved felt helpless—something we don't often feel when it comes to dealing with the police and the courts. We wanted to do something, but couldn't. Everything we thought of—writing letters, calling political officials, holding a demonstration—was either ineffectual or deemed more harmful than helpful by my friend's attorney, a brilliant African-American litigator who has seen too many of such cases. In this instance, there was nothing we could do, but the anger remained. As yet I had no idea that there was another, similar case (Darryl's) unfolding right in front of us, about which we could and would eventually do something.

WE'RE IN IT TOGETHER

During those sessions of Citizens United for Justice and at the Urban League, I also began to see that what affected African-Americans in my community also affected me. For example, to the degree that young black males, like Frank, face obstacles not of their making and consequently fall behind, get discouraged, and drop out of school, to that degree pursuing income—even illegally and violently—becomes more attractive. That response can pose a threat of the loss of life and property to everyone in the community, including me. It also means the loss of the tremendous potential that their gifts and positive contributions could make to the common good. Not only do they not contribute to the GNP and tax revenue of our local, state, and national communities, but the cost of their incarceration also drains public monies. It costs the taxpayers of North Carolina $28,000 a year to keep someone in prison. Likewise, when uninsured working-class and working-poor black and white families must go to emergency rooms for primary health-care needs, the costs of that care are passed along to all of us through increases in insurance premiums. There are also longer waits for emergency care for everyone. The result is that the uninsured move from health crisis to crisis, rather than toward a level of disease prevention and wellness that an on-going relationship with a physician would provide. "We are," as Dr. King said, "caught in an inescapable network of mutuality, tied in a single garment of destiny. Whatever affects one directly affects all indirectly."[6]

What I heard also convinced me that some of the obstacles African-Americans and working-class whites experience can only be changed in partnership with people like me. One of the reasons for the disproportionate out-of-school suspensions among African-American students is a disjunction between what a white teacher may expect in terms of classroom behavior and the usually more expressive norms of behavior young African-Americans learn in their homes and churches. Also, a white teacher interpreting silence as insolence may in other instances simply be projecting his or her fears onto an African-American student, as I had. For some of these dynamics, it becomes apparent that,

6. "Letter from Birmingham Jail," 290.

in order for them to change, white people (e.g., teachers and principals) must come to a deeper understanding of the cultural norms that shape African-American students.

The African-Americans in CUJ did not seem interested in making me feel guilty for being white or for being a professional. There were other professionals, black and white, in the group. Nor did they ask me to do anything for them. Rather they seemed to expect me to join in the various actions the group undertook and to bring along whatever resources I had at my disposal, as they were doing with the resources available to them. Maybe they knew what I was only beginning to learn: that we were all needed to change what we could so that they and their children can flourish.

The people I met there, particularly some of the African-Americans, seemed freer to express themselves emotionally and physically than the whites among whom I had grown up, and I came to see that as a good thing, thanks to insights I had gained from men's work. I loved to sing and dance growing up; yet these African-Americans seemed to have more fun in their worship services than I ever had in mine. I learned that I was missing something I didn't know I had been missing.

Finally, I also discovered that much of what I had believed about African-Americans—to the extent that I thought about them at all—was not true; it was the product of what I had been taught by others in my own communities. One example of that was what had been printed about Dr. Mendez and other black pastors in the local daily newspaper. When mentioned in the pages of the *Journal*, Reverend Mendez was almost always identified as that "activist, black pastor," evoking images of an angry, militant, aggressive figure. However, I found the African-American ministers in the group—Reverends Mendez and Carlton Eversley—were not knee-jerk militants, but deeply compassionate pastors who listened respectfully and worked tirelessly to help those who came to them. That is not to say that they and others did not get angry sometimes; they did when they saw or heard about injustices that stunted people. That made perfect sense after hearing the stories. Also, my fears of violence in the neighborhood, of hostility, of not being accepted, of feeling like an alien proved unfounded in that group. That is not to say that there are not very good reasons why African-Americans are justified in feelings of anger, resentment, and even hostility. There are. On some level I knew that. It is only to say that sentiments of that sort were not verbally expressed. In fact, in a short time, I felt very much at home at the church, in the meetings, and with people I met there.

A SOURCE OF THE FEAR

Although many of my preconceived notions and anxieties about the African-Americans I came to know at Emmanuel Baptist Church turned out to be untrue, a genealogical 1998 research trip to a state archive and a conversation with a great aunt revealed that I came by those notions and that fear honestly—through my family.

On a trip to the West Virginia state archive, I discovered that one of my ancestors had held African-Americans in slavery from the 1820s until the 1840s. I discovered a deed of trust containing the names of six people who were put up as collateral on the purchase of land. Evidently, my great-great-great-grandfather could not cover the loan payments on land he had purchased, and his creditors took him to court to recover their money. He was forced to liquidate the collateral he put up. In this case, the "collateral" was six people he owned—slaves.

This came as a surprise, because none of the other family historians had ever mentioned that anyone had owned slaves in our family, nor was there ever any reference to it in the family lore with which I was familiar. On Wednesday of that week, I called a great aunt on that side of the family tree; she lived near the archive. I asked if she had documents or pictures related to those family members I had been researching. Though I had never met her, she was very gracious and asked me to come for a visit. She offered to let me copy family documents and pictures and suggested we visit the home place of my great-great grandfather, who served as a captain in the Confederate Army. I happily accepted.

After she had invited me to visit, I mentioned on the phone that our ancestor, Nehemiah, had owned six slaves and that I knew their names. Her response was, "Well, Jim [another family historian] said that Nehemiah might have had two slaves."

"No," I said, "He had as many as six."

"Well," she replied, "many of the men in those days . . . take Robert E. Lee . . . they say he didn't believe in slavery, but he had slaves. That's just the way it was. They followed them." I presumed she meant that people like my great-great-great-grandfather followed the lead of men like Robert E. Lee.

After arriving at her home on Saturday and as we were going through pictures on her dining room table, I reiterated, "You know, Nehemiah had at least six slaves and I know their names."

She said again, "Well, Jim thought he might have had one or two."

"No, he had six," I replied.

Again, she said, "Well, Jim said he might have had one or two."

She was not hearing me, or so it seemed.

On Sunday, as I was getting ready to leave, she asked, "Steve, did you say that you know the names of Nehemiah's six slaves?" She had heard me after all.

"Yes." I said.

"What were they?"

I went to the car and got a copy of the deed of trust and read their names, "Patrick, Joseph, Henry, Sarah, Garrison, and Hannibal."

Without missing a beat, she launched into an extraordinary fifteen-minute, nearly breathless monologue that included some of the following:

"Well, I'll tell you this. I'll just tell you right now, right here. If I were growing up and I was raped by a black man and I couldn't get an abortion, I would commit suicide."

"Why?"

"Oh, I just couldn't bear the shame, oh, it would be horrible. My doctor—the one who gave me the hysterectomy [this is the same physician, she had earlier revealed, who had told her that she was "all messed up in there" and could not have children of her own] said that the way the white race was going to destroy itself was to mix with the Blacks. He said, Blacks have inferior blood—you know sickle cell anemia and all that. I believe that Blacks are inferior—in that sense I am a white supremacist. Blacks smell bad. Have you noticed? They smell when you get close to them even if they are clean—because it's the blood. There is this [black] Seventh Day Adventist who comes to my house and sits in my living room. He treats me nice and I treat him nice, but . . . he smells. And take the Bible, I don't think the Bible says that you should party and have sex with Black people."

Three or four times she interrupted this monologue to say something like: "Now I pray to my heavenly father and He says I am ok with this . . . he says I am ok with this."

After we had finished up and I was getting ready to leave, she started again: "Listen, if my son, even if he were a preacher, had sex with a Black,

I would disown him." Because she had confided earlier that the one great sadness of her life was her inability to have children, I interrupted.

"Wait a minute. Seriously, if you had a son, you would really disown him if he dated a black girl?"

She replied, "Yes. There was this girl over in Pineville named Victoria [she was related to my family] who is living with a black man up in Parkersburg. She is very pretty. She went to Concord College and started dating a black athlete. They are now living together, not married, just living together. And she will not be accepted in Pineville and she knows that. She is trash. You know what goes on at these parties, with the drugs and everything; people are around doing all kinds of things—having sex."

"Is trash having sex with someone you're not supposed to?" I asked, sitting down.

"No, it isn't that so much as having sex with a black man. Now, I don't want people to believe I am ignorant. I'm simply opinionated. I have strong opinions about mixing the races," she said.

I had always assumed that my great-great-grandfather, like many who served in the Confederate Army, fought not to protect slavery but because their friends and family expected them to. Thinking now of him and others, I asked, "Would your mom and my great-grandmother, the captain, and people of their generation have held the same opinions? Would they have had the same attitudes?"

"They'd be worse!" she exclaimed. Then she said, "I was fair to the Blacks. When I was a principal [at a middle school], at Christmas, I gave presents to the Blacks as well as the Whites. But I do not believe in mixing the races."

At one point, she said, "Oh, no. When you leave, you're going to think I'm a white supremacist."

"Well, that's what you called yourself a little while ago."

Shortly thereafter, I left. I was so struck by the conversation that I dictated what I could remember of it into a tape recorder in the car. In the next days and months, I found myself ruminating on what she might have meant by what she had said.

I told a friend about finding the deed of trust and wondered out loud, "What do you have to believe in order to buy and sell people?" It seemed surreal to me that folks whom I admire in other ways, folks who were bone of my bone and flesh of my flesh, had bought and sold people.

I had trouble trying to imagine selling my cat, much less other human beings. What did you have to believe in order for that to make sense?

In retrospect, it seemed as if I was listening to an internal tape that had been recorded in her years ago. Her monologue tumbled out fast and furiously, as if I had undone the Gordian knot that released it all.

The content of the tape is revealing. An important focus seemed to be that African-Americans are somehow different from whites, that they are not fully human (their blood is defective, they smell different). Authorities (Robert E. Lee, her physician, God) lend credibility to that assertion, and the family reinforces its "truth" by exacting adherence to it by the threat that violators will be disowned or exiled.

The purpose of the internal tape seems to have functioned to reduce the cognitive dissonance still apparent in her. That is, she professed to believe what she was saying, but acknowledged that her parents and grandparents had attitudes that were "worse" than hers. On some level, she knew that these beliefs and the slavery they justified were bad, or morally wrong; I doubt she would have wanted to be sold. Her periodic protests that God was all right with these opinions reveal her underlying anxiety that the opposite was probably true. However, she could not bear to face the excommunication that had befallen Victoria in Pineville. She both needed her family and she knew that slavery was wrong. To some extent, the stereotypes she had of blacks helped her justify why it was that her grandfather had bought and sold people: blacks, she believed, weren't really like us.

Underneath her recitation was fear, I think. She was particularly agitated when she recounted what had happened to Victoria and when she declared that she would have excommunicated a son, even a preacher son, had he been sexually involved with an African-American woman. That was particularly stunning, having come after she had shared how painful it was for her when she discovered that she could not have children. This fear of excommunication set clear limits of engagement with African-Americans in her mind. She could relate to them professionally, but never, ever socially.

When considering this aspect of her tape, I recalled an incident I had had with my father, her great nephew. When I was in high school, I had running arguments with my father about racism. On occasions when I would challenge derogatory things he said about African-Americans, we would go around and around throwing our opinions at each other.

For a time we did this fairly regularly, without a great deal of animosity. One exchange felt different. We had had what seemed to me like a fairly routine argument. As I left the kitchen, he said with more than the usual feeling, "If you ever bring a black girl in this house, that's it!" It was the only time I ever remember my dad threatening me, for that was the way it felt. Yet the threat seemed to come out of the blue; we hadn't been talking about interracial marriage, or even dating, and then—boom—out this comes. Now, it makes sense. Becoming involved with someone of another race was the line his family drew in the sand. It was the transgression for which he could have been excommunicated and for which he apparently was prepared to excommunicate me. And it seemed to have the desired effect on me. Thinking back on my high school experience, I recall that I knew several black guys on my basketball team, but I cannot remember the name of one black girl at my school.

What strikes me about this is the long-term stubborn persistence of beliefs and behaviors that enabled people to justify the practice of slavery. What begins in an historical moment to justify the mistreatment of a group of people persists, even when the reason the stereotypes were formulated no longer exists. It seems the last time anyone in this branch of my family held someone in slavery was in the 1840s, when Nehemiah defaulted on the loan and passed the ownership of Patrick, Joseph, Henry, Sarah, Garrison, and Hannibal to others. However, in my family and many others like it, these stereotypes have reinforced our social isolation from African-Americans for at least six generations.

These stereotypes and consequent isolation have been instilled and enforced by the manipulation of one of the most elemental of human needs—the need to belong and the consequent fear of excommunication. The particular need to belong to a family is centrally related to our instinct for survival. As mammals, we will die if we are not cared for as infants. Being threatened with being exiled from our families is terrifying. Even in adulthood, long after our almost complete physical dependency is over, we maintain an emotional and physical need for belonging and acceptance. It is the manipulation of this central human need by our families, churches, or other groups on whom we depend and with which we identify that is so insidious. The need to belong is used to exclude others from the family or group or one faces exclusion oneself.[7]

7. Similar incidents experienced by a wide variety of whites he interviewed led Thandeka, *Learning to be White*, to identify white shame as a result of having to deny, or

Another thing that strikes me about this exchange is the fact that at some level my aunt knew that what she believed and how she acted toward blacks was wrong. It reminds me of one of the reasons for the fear I felt driving over to Emmanuel Baptist Church. At some level, I knew that black people had good reasons to resent and maybe even hate me for the way I and other whites treated them.

IT'S *MY* BUSINESS?

Several years ago this was poignantly illustrated by Jane Elliott, the first-grade teacher from Arkansas who developed for her students an exercise called "Blue Eyes/Brown Eyes." In the exercise, students with blue eyes are arbitrarily stereotyped as less smart, less disciplined, less worthy than those with brown eyes. The students with brown eyes are given special privileges and treated as though they are smarter, more disciplined, and generally better than the blue-eyed children. After a week, the roles are reversed. The point is to teach them about the nature and effects of mis-treatment directed at people on the basis of some characteristic unrelated to their character. The effects—even after only a week—are devastating on the group targeted for treatment as inferiors. They become anxious, depressed, and perform less well in their school work.

At a presentation before nine hundred students during orientation at Wake Forest, she asked the audience of mostly white student, faculty, and staff, "Everyone who would like to be treated the way African-Americans are systematically treated in this country raise your hand. [Pause—no hands went up.] I don't think you understood me, everyone who would like to be treated the way African-Americans are treated in this country please raise your hands." [Pause. Still no hands were raised.] And then she said, "Well, you've told me something. You know what is going on. Now tell me what you are doing about it."

Many of us whites in the room knew that African-Americans are still systematically mistreated in ways that we do not want to be. Even after the gains of the Civil Rights Movement, most whites enjoy signifi-cant social privileges, hold assumptions of cultural superiority, and wield more economic power than the majority of African-Americans. And we know that these realities continue to shape and distort the lives of African-Americans in destructive ways.

---

repress, authentic feelings as being one of the core elements of white racism.

There was an elephant in my city that I knew about at some level but that I opted not to look at too closely. Presumably my colleague, Alton Pollard, knew that and invited me to look anyway. What I began to see was that race was not just something that African-Americans have. I have a racial identity too, and it carries with it certain assumptions and beliefs about myself and about African-Americans and that shapes my behavior toward them. Those, in turn, contribute to the larger, institutional dynamics that limit opportunities and resources available to them for their flourishing. As a white, my racial identity has been shaped and transmitted to me by other whites, particularly those I love and who love me. And I began to see that racism and its effects are not just the concern of African-Americans; they are my business, too.

four

"Somebody Was Listening":
Hunt's Miraculous Release

October 16, 2000—the day Darryl learned that the U.S. Supreme Court declined to hear his appeal—was a dark one for Darryl. Yet there was a glimmer of light and love: he got married the next day to April Clark, Imam Khalid Grigg's stepdaughter.

April had met Darryl in 1989 when he was out on bond and lived with the Griggs. She was a student and needed help with her two-year-old daughter. She was impressed with Darryl's quiet and gentle spirit, and they became friends. By 1997, she had divorced. Without telling her stepfather, she found Darryl's address and started writing to Darryl. Soon she began visiting with her three children. When he found out about it, Imam Griggs discouraged the relationship; he believed that women should not marry incarcerated men, but should wait until the man got out and established himself. April moved ahead anyway, and by 2000 she and Darryl had decided to marry. His appeal was still with the Supreme Court. They set October 17 as their wedding date. Then, Darryl got the news on October 16. He spent an anxious day and night waiting for April to come to the Piedmont Correctional Institution in Salisbury. He was afraid that when she heard the news that the Supreme Court had declined to hear his appeal she wouldn't want to marry him. He didn't know if he would ever get out of prison.

When April got to the visitation room, Darryl told her about the Court's decision. She responded, "What's that got to do with us?"

He said, "I may never get out of prison."

"Darryl, if I can't have you in this life—physically, here—I'd have you in the next life."

So, they got married, as planned, in the prison visitation room.

"That was the best day of my life," Darryl said later.[1]

RABIL KEEPS HOPE ALIVE

After Judge Morgan's decision that the exclusion of Darryl's DNA evidence would not have made any difference in a third trial, Jim Ferguson and attorney Ben Dowling-Sendor worried about Mark Rabil. He had become withdrawn. After catching up with him, they talked and decided to file an appeal to the NC Supreme Court. The hard part, said Rabil, was writing the letter to Darryl. He tried to sound positive:

> Dear Darryl,
>
> I think I broke my hand when I slammed it on the courthouse door as I left after my brief statement to the press. So, it will probably be a long time before I stop feeling this day. I went to the YMCA and ran one mile for each year of this case in the wind and rain. We will not give up, we will be successful, you will be released. As long as you are shackled, so are we. Remember what Moses said to Israel before the Red Sea was parted, "The Lord, Himself, will fight for you. You have only to keep still."[2]

While Darryl stayed still, Mark did not.

After the U.S. Supreme Court decision, Rabil and Ferguson made one more attempt to free Darryl. They submitted a Petition for Commutation to Governor Jim Hunt's office in December 2000. District Attorney Tom Keith opposed the petition. Deborah Sykes's mother, Evelyn Jefferson, ran a campaign in her Chattanooga, TN, church that produced three hundred letters to Governor Hunt opposing clemency for Darryl.[3] The governor

1. Stern and Sunberg, *Trials of Darryl Hunt*, 1:19:07.

2. Ibid., 1:10:29.

3. Mrs. Jefferson had hired a private investigator to look into the circumstances of Deborah's death; she was particularly concerned that the police dispatcher had sent the squad car to the wrong fire station, after Johnny Gray's 911 call and her daughter's body was not found until seven hours after the assault. Through the trials, she became convinced of Hunt's guilt.

left office in 2003 without acting on the petition. Mike Easley, the state's Attorney General during the 1993–94 appeals process, succeeded Hunt in the governor's office, so it seemed very unlikely that he would be favorably disposed toward the Petition.

"As hopeless as this case seemed, Mark [Rabil] wouldn't give up,"[4] Jim Ferguson observed later.

So, in January 2003, Rabil withdrew the Commutation Petition from Easley's desk and hatched the idea to file a motion in Superior Court to compare the DNA in the Sykes case to a database of 35,000 DNA profiles of convicted felons stored in the SBI files in Raleigh. He said he was trying to "keep hope alive" and knew that it was up to the defense team to solve the case if Darryl were ever to go free. Ferguson and others thought it was like looking for a needle in a haystack. District Attorney Tom Keith did not object.

On April 8, Judge Anderson Cromer ruled in favor of the motion and the sample from the Sykes rape kit went to the SBI lab in Raleigh.

ZERWICK'S INVESTIGATIVE SERIES

When Rabil filed the motion and Cromer ruled, Carl Crothers, the Executive Editor of the *Winston-Salem Journal*, decided to commission an investigative series on the case. Crothers had come to Winston-Salem from Tampa for the job seven years earlier in 1996. To get the lay of the land, he had at the time asked his staff to name the most important stories that had shaped the community. One of those stories was the Deborah Sykes/Darryl Hunt story. He asked for clippings on the case, and they brought him boxes full. He noticed that the paper had reported what the police and prosecutors said and how the defense team and Defense Committee responded, but that the *Journal* had never done its own investigation to test those claims or put them in a context for its readers. He had planned to do the series back in 1998, but other senior staff had dissuaded him, arguing that Hunt had been convicted twice and the story was dead. When Rabil filed the motion in 2003, Crothers saw a hook. He believed Phoebe Zerwick—a special assignment writer—to be the best-equipped journalist on the staff to tackle it. He called her and asked her if she would do it, and she agreed.[5]

4. Stern and Sunberg, *Trials of Darryl Hunt*, 1:19:18.

5. Interview with Carl Crothers, interview by author, June 2, 2004.

Mark Rabil gave her about 20,000 pages to read. The three months she thought the project would take turned into seven months. She knew that the case had divided the community along racial lines, with black people having one view and white people a very different one. Since the views were so entrenched on both sides, she believed that, if the newspaper stepped back and presented the facts, stripped of the rhetoric, the community might be helped. So Zerwick started reading the documents provided by Rabil and doing her own interviews of officers and witnesses who had been involved in the various investigations that had taken place. The eight-part series, "Murder, Race, Justice" appeared daily, from Sunday, November 16 through Sunday, November 23, 2003.[6]

The series triggered several events.

While the series was still running, Zerwick called Rabil and said that she would like to include something about the DNA test and asked if he had heard anything. Rabil called the lab asking about the progress of the tests. The technician responded,

"We've already shown it wasn't Darryl Hunt's, what more do you want?"

"Well, we want to know whose it is."[7]

Judge Cromer was reading the series that week when Rabil called him to say that the SBI lab had not yet done the DNA comparisons. The judge called the lab and threatened the SBI with contempt of court unless the comparison was done.

Reverend Mendez, Chair of the Hunt Defense Committee, who lived in one of the city's suburbs, reported that one of his white neighbors had come to him and commiserated about what a bad deal Darryl had gotten from the system.

> And suddenly I knew then that something was happening—something good, something different—it justified what we had been saying for 20 years. We kept moving, but we didn't realize what was about to unfold.[8]

---

6. See the website for the series and related documents and photographs: http://darrylhunt.journalnow.com/

7. Stern and Sunberg, *Trials of Darryl Hunt*, 1:24:01.

8. Ibid., 1:21:56.

IT'S MY BUSINESS

I was among the white people to whom something started happening at this point. One day back in the summer, out of the blue, Rev. Mendez said to me, "You know we need to get back on this thing about Darryl." He had never said much to me about it before that. I asked him about the case, and we talked a bit about it. Then, I put it out of my mind—until the newspaper series by Zerwick began in November. I began reading the series that very first Sunday. As I read, I found the parallels with what my basketball-playing friend, Geoff, had experienced striking. Detectives were trying to close a case; they conducted suggestive, leading photo lineups to encourage a witness to pick out the photo of their "suspect." Then, once a witness had picked out a photo, matching the person in the photo to the person in a live lineup is almost automatic. Then, that person becomes, in the mind of the witness, the person they saw that day. It is exactly what happened to Geoff. I called my friend and pastor, Richard Groves of Wake Forest Baptist Church, on Tuesday and asked, "Are you reading this stuff?" He said yes. The rest of the week, I took a highlighter and went through the articles trying to figure out who killed Mrs. Sykes. I'd call Richard and we'd compare notes, trying to solve the mystery. Looking back on it, it was pretty ridiculous—these ordinary, lay citizens trying to solve a murder from what we read in the newspaper; the point was, we were hooked by the injustice of it all, and had begun to understand how Mark Rabil must have felt. Solving the case and finding the killer constituted the only way Darryl was going to be freed and justice done for Deborah Sykes.

On Monday, the day after the series started, Mary Lane, a seventy-three-year-old white woman, called Zerwick at the paper and said that she had never believed that Darryl Hunt killed Debbie Sykes. Her daughter-in-law had been assaulted and raped about the same time, and she was convinced that those two attacks were connected. Zerwick remembered a case in her research in which a single black man had kidnapped and raped a young white woman near where Mrs. Sykes had been attacked. She went to the police department and asked to see the file on the "Integon Rape." The survivor was Regina K. Zerwick learned that police had not followed up on her identification of Willard Brown as the likely perpetrator back in 1986. She came back to the office with the news. Excited, Executive Editor Crothers couldn't believe that the police had never compared the two cases. But Zerwick did some more research and was told by the police that the perpetrator couldn't have been Brown because he had been in prison the day Sykes was murdered. She and Crothers were disappointed, but she included the story in the last installment of the series as an example of a lead that hadn't been followed. "I just thought it was an interesting twist that we ought to put in there just in case."[9]

The following week at the Ministers' Conference of Winston-Salem and Vicinity, Rev. Eversley—spokesperson for the Hunt Defense Committee—reported that, in light of the *Journal* series, Larry Little had called for a rally at Lloyd's Presbyterian Church.[10] The Committee wanted to demand the release of Darryl. After his report, I asked Rev. Mendez, then serving as President of the Conference, for the floor. I said that I and other white people in the community had been reading the series and wanted to help. Dr. Serenus Churn, pastor of the Mt. Zion Baptist Church, rose to say that those whites who wanted to help should be welcomed. Rev. Mendez asked Eversley to arrange a meeting for me with Larry Little. We met at the IHOP on Peter's Creek Parkway. On the way over, I was apprehensive. I had never met Little; all I knew of him was what I had read about him in the newspaper or heard from others—he was the founder of the Black Panther Party, a vocal critic of the Police Department, and had once stood with a rifle on the porch of an elderly black woman to stop her eviction from her house. The paper had run the picture at the time and several times since. When I got to the IHOP, Rev. Eversley introduced us, and I slid into one side of a long booth; Little slid in beside me. At first, Little was cautious—he didn't turn towards me or look me in the eye. Then, as we talked about the case and I mentioned several things that seemed outrageous about the detectives' behavior, he began to turn toward me. He was one of the most passionate, engaging, empathic people I had ever met. By the end of the ninety-minute breakfast, I was a part of the Defense Committee. I asked what I and others could do. He told me to call Mark Rabil, so I did.

We met for lunch on December 17. By this time, Rabil had lost his private practice; clients were skittish about his very public "political" profile. By 2003, he was in the Capital Defender's Office. He brought to lunch with him his assistant, Mike Klinkosum. We talked about a strategy, using Zerwick's series to get more widespread support from white people for

9. Ibid., 1:23:25.

10. The Ministers' Conference of Winston-Salem and Vicinity is a predominantly African-American organization made up of pastors of churches in Winston-Salem and surrounding counties.

another commutation petition and about the ways women clergy might make contact with Mrs. Jefferson to ask for her support.

MAKING IT THEIR BUSINESS: THE DNA "HIT"

In early December, the SBI ran the test on the DNA sample from the Sykes case. The geneticist was able to get good resolution of nine loci or sites on the DNA strand and seven of them matched the DNA profile of a person in the state database of violent felons. North Carolina law requires that at least ten sites of the possible fifteen sites be clear. If there are ten clear sites and only seven match another profile, the matter is settled: there is no official identification and the testing ends. In this case, since there was only clear resolution of nine, not ten, sites, the rule didn't apply. The geneticist knew of a lab in Alabama, known for its technique in the testing process, that might be able to get a clear resolution of more sites and, thereby, definitively rule the database profile in or out. The decision was made to fly the samples to Alabama.

On December 12, the SBI called WSPD Chief Linda Davis and informed her that seven of the sites on the DNA from the Sykes sample matched the profile of an Anthony Brown. In the meantime, Chief Davis assigned Detective Mike Rowe to work with SBI agent Scott Williams on an investigation. While waiting for the test results, Rowe and Williams located Anthony Brown in Winston-Salem. He had been released from prison July 14, 2003, after serving sixteen years for a sexual offense.[11] Detective Rowe also looked at old case files of assaults on women in the mid-1980s. Prompted by Zerwicks's recent inquiry, he looked at the Regina K. file. There he saw that she had, in 1986 and again in 1987, identified Willard Brown as her assailant. He checked Department of Correction records and discovered that, despite what Brown had said and Detective Crump had repeated to Zerwick, Brown was not in prison on August 10, 1984; he had been released on June 13 or in the early morning hours of June 14.[12]

The results came back on Tuesday, December 16. The lab had indeed been able to produce better resolution and, therefore, the comparison of more sites. However, those markers made clear that Anthony Brown was not a match. But the lab suggested that, due to the high number of shared sites, the DNA profile in the Sykes case might be that of a relative of Brown.

11. Sykes Report, 30 n. 144.
12. Sykes Report, 51–52.

Willard Brown was Anthony Brown's brother. Rowe checked and Willard happened to be in Forsyth County jail serving a sixty-day sentence on a parole violation. He was slated for release Monday, December 22. Rowe took Brown into an interview room and asked him about the Sykes murder. Brown denied knowing anything about it. Rowe laid a pack of cigarettes on the table and left the room. While he was gone, Brown smoked two of the cigarettes. Later, Rowe bagged the butts and sent them to the lab in Alabama for DNA testing of the saliva.

Mark Rabil had been informed of these developments on Wednesday, December 17. According to him, a conference call with Judge Cromer, the Attorney General's Office, and DA Tom Keith produced an agreement that, when the DNA results came back, no one would talk to the press about it until the four had had another conversation. They were concerned that if there was a match, the suspect be properly questioned. Given the state's history of offers of reward money, plea bargains, promises of cutting jail time for snitches, and intimidation of witnesses in the case, Rabil wanted to make sure that any interrogations would be transparent and focused on the truth—not on defending the state's convoluted theories of the case.

On Friday, December 19, the lab called Chief Davis. There was an identical, full match to the DNA in Mrs. Sykes's rape kit. It was Willard Brown.

The Attorney General's Office called Mark Rabil and told him. Mark immediately called Larry Little.

"Larry, brace yourself. This is it. They have found the murderer. We got the DNA. It's over; Darryl's is going to be free!"

"Mark, cut this bullshit out. You are always talkin' this shit and then we get f——— over. I'm not going on this emotional roller coaster with you."

"No, Larry, look . . . ."

"Mark stop all this bullshit; calm down. This is still racist Winston-f——— Salem; this is racist North Carolina. You've done this s—before. So, stop it."

"Larry, wait, listen to me. The DNA came back with a hit."[13]

IT'S STILL NOT OVER

Little's suspicions, it turned out, were justified. Chief Davis called the District Attorney Keith who, despite his agreement with Rabil, Judge

13. Stern and Sunberg, *Trials of Darryl Hunt*, 1:25:04–1:25:49.

Cromer, and the Attorney General's Office, held a brief press conference that evening on the steps of the Hall of Justice.[14] Saturday morning, the *Journal* ran the story. Keith said that yet another person had been identified in the Sykes murder. "We've all known that there's a third person since 1994," he said. "This is that third person." The DA had returned to the theory, developed after the 1994 DNA exclusion, that, along with Hunt and Mitchell implicated by the three new witnesses during the second trial, the state finally had the missing rapist—the third accomplice—in custody. Rabil was livid. He believed that, by going directly to the press, Keith was trying once again to manipulate public opinion about the case rather than pursuing the new evidence fairly. The only person ever to be linked to the case through material evidence had not even been interviewed at this point, and yet Keith was arguing publicly that the third person has been identified. "This shows that Keith . . . has still got tunnel vision. They're trying to prove a theory that has been proven wrong time and again." As Rev. Eversley pointed out, the Prosecutor Dean Bowman had indicted both Hunt and Mitchell before the second trial and argued that the state's own witness, Johnny Gray, had probably been involved. So, according to the state's latest theory, Brown should have been the fourth suspect. Further, Rabil had talked with the attorney general's office late Friday. "My understanding from the attorney general's office is there's no evidence of any connection with Darryl Hunt or Sammy Mitchell. Therefore, this should end [any theory involving Hunt or Mitchell] and begin the prosecution of the real killer."[15]

Keith's tactics fed the worst fears of the Hunt Defense Committee and Rabil:

> Now we don't know what's going on. We don't know the name of the suspect, we don't where he is, we don't know if he's been interviewed. We don't know if he has an attorney, we don't know if the interview was recorded, we don't know if any promises of leniency were made, [or] if he (the new suspect) pointed the finger at Darryl Hunt or Sammy Mitchell.[16]

Given the cozy relationship between the DA's office and the WSPD detectives in the case, it was easy to imagine that they might offer Brown a deal,

14. Keith claimed later that there was no agreement with Rabil, Cromer, and the AG's office. Wilson and Hewlett, "DA defends handling of new suspect in death."

15. Zerwick, "New suspect in Hunt case."

16. Ibid.

specifically that they might take the death penalty off the table if Brown would implicate Darryl and Sammy. It had been done before.

Little called a strategy meeting for 9:00 a.m. on Saturday morning. Rev. Eversley called at 7:30 a.m. and asked if I would call other whites who wanted to help. I called Dr. Groves and Chris Baumann. We converged with Little, Eversley, Khalid Griggs, Rev. Willard Bass, and Mark Rabil at the Peter's Creek IHOP. Larry had Darryl on his cell phone. Mark reviewed the events of the last week. The group fretted about what to do. We were worried about Keith making a deal with Brown. At one point, Little asked Darryl, who had been listening on speaker phone, what he thought we should do. Darryl responded, "Larry, let's trust in God. He's led us this far. He'll lead us the rest of the way." The ordained clergy folks looked around at each other sheepishly; in the face of this kind of faith, our anxiety seemed a little embarrassing. But we kept on planning. We decided to have two press conferences; a white one at 12:30 p.m. at Wake Forest Baptist Church and a black one at 2:00 p.m. at Emmanuel Baptist. Rev. Eversley called the media.

Chris and I hopped in our cars and called as many white clergy as we could think of, asking them to come to Wake Forest as soon as they could; we needed to write a statement.

White Clergy Press Conference Credit © 2003 *Winston-Salem Journal* photo by Megan Morr

We worked on that statement and had fifteen ministers to meet the press at 12:30 in front of Wait Chapel on campus. Richard Groves and Laura

Spangler, pastor of Lloyd Presbyterian Church, read the statement. It declared:

> In this Advent season, we, who are clergy of the Prince of Peace, feel compelled to speak out on behalf of justice for our community.
>
> The Darryl Hunt case has been one of the most racially divisive episodes in the history of our city. Now for the first time in nearly 20 years we have scientific evidence that should lead to truth, justice and, therefore, healing for the family of Deborah Sykes, the family and friends of Darryl Hunt and for our whole community. In order to obtain the truth and justice that will lead to that healing, what is needed is a fair and impartial investigation of this case by an independent agency.[17]

As justification for the independent investigation—insulated from the district attorney's office—the group stated that DA Keith was "following the mistakes and injustices of the past." After the 1994 DNA exclusions of Hunt and Mitchell, the district attorney had "failed to conduct an investigation to identify Deborah Sykes' rapist." We didn't specify the "independent agency," because we didn't have much confidence in the previous investigation conducted by the SBI, but didn't know who else to suggest. Three television affiliates, the campus NPR affiliate, the *Journal*, and the *Winston-Salem Chronicle* covered the press conference.

Later, at Emmanuel Baptist Church, Rev. Eversley read a statement to the same press corps calling for Hunt's unconditional release, because the new DNA evidence should end his "19-year nightmare of unjust, unfair, inaccurate and racist incarceration" for a crime he didn't commit.

> The hands of the police and prosecution in this case now drip with the blood of Mrs. Sykes. [They] are stained with the semen of the mysterious Mr. X, whose DNA directly matches that found in Mrs. Sykes, and their lips have leaked a series of lies, manipulations, falsities and innuendos for almost two decades.[18]

Rev. Mendez said, "Our plea to Mr. Keith is that there is a life at stake here that is worth more than the power struggle. The only scientific evidence

---

17. Personal copy of the press statement. Among those present and pictured on page 80 are (l-r): Reverends Lynn Rhoades, Sid Kelly, Laura Spangler, Albert C. Winn, Steve Boyd, Richard Groves, Fred Horton, Peggy Matthews, Susan Parker, Chris Baumann, and Jeff Coppage.

18. Hinton, "Evidence Stirs Some Angry Reactions."

that has been presented is this DNA testing. It seems to have worked for everyone else in the country; what is it about Winston-Salem?"[19]

As the conference broke up and the press members left to file their stories, Rabil's assistant, Mike Clinkosum, rushed into the sanctuary. He had been on the phone with a public defender, who told him that he had been barred from seeing Brown due to an order by the jail captain that prohibited visitors. Again, the Defense Committee feared the possibility of manipulation by the DA. We each took a share of the names of the media members who had just left and called them to relay the news. Several reporters went to the jail and reported on that development. "I've never been denied access to see a client, or a potential client," Brown's public defender said. "We were his lawyers in a case that was recently disposed." Rabil complained to the *Journal*, "The way we read that is, they don't want Darryl Hunt's attorneys or investigators . . . to talk to [Brown] and find out what's going on."[20] Forsyth County Sheriff Bill Schatzmen lifted the order late Saturday evening.[21]

Monday morning, we had another strategy session at Emmanuel. Mayor Allen Joines joined a group of twenty people with equal numbers of blacks and whites.[22] We shared with him our lack of confidence in the police department's Criminal Investigation Division, as well as in the DA's office. One of the white clergy expressed our hope that Winston-Salem was a part of the New South, rather than the Old South dynamics that had been a part of the city's history. Rev. Mendez observed that, for the city to move ahead with the recruitment of new employers to replace the decimated textile and tobacco industries, we had to deal with the blatant examples of racism that still plagued us. Another white pastor expressed the wish that Winston-Salem avoid the kinds of public racial tensions and clashes that had recently damaged Cincinnati.[23]

19. Stern and Sunberg, "Trials of Darryl Hunt," 1:29:30–51.

20. Wilson and Hewlitt, "DA Defends Handling of New Suspect in Death."

21. The Forsyth Sheriff's Department supervises the jail. Zerwick, "New Suspect, New Clues."

22. Among the African-Americans present were Larry Little, Reverend Mendez, Rev. Eversley, Imam Griggs, Rev. Dr. A.T. Griffey, Rev. Dr. Simeon Ilesanmi, and Rev. Willard Bass. The whites included Reverend Steve McCutchan, Hoppy Elliott, Rev. Hal Hayek, Rev. Lynn Rhoades, and Chris Baumann.

23. Violence rocked Cincinnati April 9–14, 2001, when an unarmed black teenager was shot and killed by a police officer. Civil rights leaders protested the deaths of fifteen young black males at the hands of the police.

Mayor Joines asked what he could do. We suggested that he call for an independent investigation by the SBI and that he arrange a meeting of the group with Tom Keith. After he left, the group made tentative plans for a demonstration at the jail for Tuesday, the following day. Later, Larry Little commented on the atmosphere of the city at the time, saying, "If they pulled some mess this time, the community probably would explode and, this time, it wouldn't just be with the black community exploding."[24]

Mayor Joines spoke with City Council members that evening and released a statement saying that they planned to make a formal request that the SBI conduct a probe into the recent developments in the case. Joines said that he was doing so not as any criticism of the police department, but in order to "restore public confidence that the case will be fairly prosecuted," adding that, "I think there is an opportunity here for the community to heal itself."[25]

Also that evening, Mayor Joines called Rev. Mendez and said that there were some helpful developments and asked for patience. Tom Keith called Larry Little:

"I think I can resolve this case. I think I can come up with something for everybody."

"Well, Tom, I'm not interested in something for everybody; I'm interested in justice for Darryl Hunt."

"You may get what you want," Keith responded.

"With that, I'll give you twenty-four hours."[26]

WILLARD BROWN CONFESSES

Unbeknownst to the Defense Committee and the public, Detectives Rowe and Williams had interviewed Brown over the weekend and he had denied any involvement in Mrs. Sykes's murder. He was scheduled to be released at noon on Monday. Rowe went to him around 11:00 a.m. and said that they had the DNA evidence and arrested him and charged him with the murder of Deborah Sykes. As officers took him for the booking, Brown broke down and started crying.

24. Stern and Sunberg, *Trials of Darryl Hunt*, 1:29:20–29.
25. Zerwick and Hewlett, "A REQUEST: Mayor Wants SBI to Handle Probe."
26. Stern and Sunberg, *Trials of Darryl Hunt*, 1:29:55–1:30:14.

"I apologize to Darryl Hunt. Tell Sammy Mitchell I'm sorry. And tell the Sykes family that I'm sorry."

Rowe and Williams said, "What are you talking about?"

Brown confessed to the crime. The detectives took him to the scene of the crime, and he described what had happened. Everything he said agreed with the earliest statements by Hooper and Murphy with the exception that he claimed that he had committed the act alone. Although William Hooper said he saw two black men with Mrs. Sykes that morning, Brown said no one else helped him.

On Tuesday, the Defense Committee and other Hunt supporters waited for word of Darryl's release. Mark Rabil's wife, Judy, convinced him to fly home from a family vacation, "You need to be there for closure," she told him.[27] We had been told that Darryl would be released at 4:00 p.m. As afternoon turned to evening, tempers flared and plans were made again for a demonstration at the jail for Wednesday.

Darryl had been moved earlier that day from the Randolph Correctional Center in Asheboro to the Forsyth County Jail. The delay resulted from a trip Rowe and Williams had made to Raleigh, where they had spent all day Tuesday polygraphing Brown to see if they could find any record that Hunt and Brown knew each other. Word came finally from the DA's office that Hunt would not be released that day. Everyone went home. Around midnight, Rowe and Williams telephoned Keith, informing him that they could find no evidence of a relationship between Brown and Hunt.[28]

"DARRYL HUNT IS FREE!"

At 7:30 a.m. the next morning, Christmas Eve, Rabil and Klinkosum received word that Darryl would be released between 10:00 a.m. and 11:00 a.m. They called around and asked that we spread the word and get people to gather at Emmanuel Baptist Church.

Just after 11:00, Darryl signed papers related to his release, "I was signing it thinking, 'They're going to come and snatch it back.'" When Darryl's wife April got the call from Imam Griggs, she was getting ready to visit Darryl—as always—at Forsyth County Jail. She collected some clothes for him—a new leather jacket and a borrowed sports coat, if that

27. Gura and Zerwick, "New Clues Throw Out Long-Held Theories."
28. Zerwick, "Keith to Plea for a Hunt Pardon."

didn't fit—and took them to the jail.[29] A reporter caught her in the lobby of the jail and asked her how she felt when she first heard he would be released. She responded breathlessly, "Like right now, I have butterflies—and just excited . . . and praying, praying that this will actually really be it this morning," touching her head scarf.

"How long have you waited for this day?"

"Ohhhh . . . years. Since the day I met him," she said, a smile spreading across her face.

Darryl changed from a white prison uniform to the new slacks, shirt, and sports coat. Then, at 11:50 a.m. on December 24, 2003, Darryl Hunt walked down a long hall and through a door, where he met April, put his arms around her and lifted her off the floor. Outside, he could hear chants, "Darryl Hunt is free! Darryl Hunt is free!"

Darryl emerges from Forsyth County Jail accompanied by Sheriff Bill Schatzman. Credit: © 2003, *Winston-Salem Journal*, photo by Megan Morr

Larry Little came over to embrace him, saying, "Yes! Yes! Yes!"

29. Zerwick, "HE IS FREE: Hunt Gives Thanks to His Supporters."

Darryl received by (l-r) Khalid Griggs, Carlton Eversley, James Ferguson, Larry Little, Mike Klinkosum, and Mark Rabil. Credit:© 2003 *Winston-Salem Journal* by Jennifer Rotenizer

After too many years, John Mendez, Carlton Eversley, and Khalid Griggs took turns hugging Darryl.

"It's a long time coming, man," James Ferguson said.[30]

Then, the group, led by Darryl and April, with Larry at their side, came through the doors into the fresh air and bright sunshine; cameras, microphones, and chants of "Darryl Hunt is free; Darryl Hunt is free" met them, as reporters crowded on the stairs in front of them.

Darryl and April greet supporters. Credit: © 2003, *Winston-Salem Journal* photo by Megan Morr

30. Ibid.

"How do you feel, Darryl?"

"I don't believe there are words to express how I feel right now," Darryl said.

"Darryl, what about Willard Brown, the man who let you languish in prison for nineteen years, knowing that he was responsible?"

"I don't dwell on him, or try to figure out why he did what he did, or anything like that. God willing, he will get a fair trial."

"The District Attorney says you may still not be exonerated. Do you feel that that will come to pass; that you will be set free for good?"

"Yes."

"Why is that?"

Darryl smiled, "Faith in God and the fact that I am innocent."

The group got in a van and drove to the Community Mosque, where it was time for the day's second prayer. After prayer, he spoke to the men, "I never gave up faith that one day I would be here."[31]

The group at Emmanuel had started gathering at 9:30. It was a mixture of folks—mostly African-Americans—who had been involved in the struggle for almost two decades and others—black and white—who had gotten involved more recently, as I had. We told stories of how we had gotten involved with Darryl, or Larry, or Mark, sang hymns, and prayed. Joycelyn Johnson, a City Council member, played the piano. Larry Womble, a State Representative and long-time faithful leader of the Defense Committee, was outside on his cell phone, relaying news about events as they happened at the Forsyth County Jail.

When word spread that the van had arrived, the number of people had swelled to two hundred, and the chant started, "Darryl Hunt is free! Darryl Hunt is free!" Darryl and April walked through the narthex and down the aisle, stopping to greet people.

I stood in the narthex, to the side. Larry brought Darryl and April over and introduced me to them. I felt more at home than at any time in my life.

"EVERYBODY CAN HEAL FROM THIS"

They made their way to the front of the sanctuary to a long table that had been set up for Larry, Mark, Rev. Mendez, Rev. Eversley, Imam Griggs, and Nelson Malloy, a City Council member, who had been active on the

31. Ibid.

defense team from the beginning. Those of us on the Defense Committee —about thirty strong—sat behind them. The moderator, Rev. Eversley, introduced everyone and then called on "the man of the hour" to speak.

Darryl rose and said, "First, I want to thank God. God is the only one who could bring justice in this case.

"I want also to remember some people who are not here. Mrs. [Mattie] Mitchell [Sammy's mother who had been a second mother to Darryl] has gone on, but she believed in me and she should be here now.

"I want to start out with Larry," his voice shaking.

"Take your time Darryl, it's all right."

Darryl Hunt, April Hunt, and Imam Griggs at the press conference. Credit: © 2003, Winston-Salem Journal photo by Bruce Chapman

"In the beginning, he asked me was I innocent? Did I do the crime? And I told him, 'No,' and he said, 'If you didn't I will fight for you, but if you did I will fight against you.'

"It was that that helped me feel at peace and he has been with me through these nineteen years. He is a blessing from God because at that point when I was arrested they probably could have shot me and gotten it over with and there wouldn't have been nothing said. The hell that I experienced the first couple of days . . . but after Larry became interested I was a little more at peace. I felt a little bit better, safer is the word I'm looking for."

He thanked Mark Rabil for sticking with him throughout the years at great cost to himself and his family.

Mark Rabil and Larry Little at the press conference. Credit: © 2003, Winston-Salem Journal photo by Bruce Chapman

He spoke about the sermons of Reverends Mendez and Eversley that had given him strength. The fact that they were Christian and he was a Muslim didn't matter, "The word of God is everywhere," he said. "His truth shines."[32]

Further, he said, "We can all—as one, black, white—everybody can heal from this and grow, so we won't be separated by race. Injustice can happen to anybody. And if we are separated by race, there is always going to be someone locked in prison. I just pray that we, together, not allow this to happen to anyone else."

After his statement, reporters began to ask Darryl questions.

"Mr. Hunt, you don't seem angry. Are you angry at all?"

"Years ago, when I first went to prison, an older man told me that anger will kill you from the inside. I don't want to die; I want to live. And if I say that I believe in God and God has said that everything would be ok, then, who am I angry at? Because nothing happens to man without

32. Zerwick, Hewlett and Garber, "I Always Had Faith."

God's hands; so, God has a reason, so if I get angry or bitter, then I've got to be getting angry and bitter with God. And I won't do that, because God blessed me."

When asked about the Sykes family, Darryl responded:

> Now that we are going to get some justice, real justice, I'm hoping and praying that they [Deborah Sykes's family] can get peace. Their experience is just as painful as mine. That hurt me, because I am innocent and there was nothing I could do. I pray the justice will be done and everybody can get peace now.

After about a half an hour, the questions slowed, and those from the Defense Committee who wanted to speak did so.

Then, Darryl and April left to go home—a house Darryl had only seen in pictures: "I'm just curious to know how it's going to feel to walk in the door," Hunt said.[33]

At the beginning of the day, I had called a young friend from church, Francois Byers, to tell him, "Darryl is getting out of jail today. If you want to go, get ready and I'll pick you up in ten minutes." He did and I did. At the end of the day, as I drove him home, I asked, "Well, what did you think?"

He said, "I'll never forget the look on Darryl's face when he came in the church."

"Why? How did he look?"

"It was pure joy."

It was—joy for him and for the many others who were blessed to be present.

"SOMEBODY WAS LISTENING"

There was one final legal hurdle. The court had docketed Rabil's Motion for Appropriate Relief for February 6, 2004, with Judge Andy Cromer presiding.

Rev. Eversley told a reporter, "We don't have any right to trust the system, to do the right thing. So, we must—as Thomas Jefferson said— remain eternally vigilant—that on February 6, Darryl gets what he has always deserved—total vindication, total exoneration—an apology."

The evening before the hearing, Darryl said, "We want to plan for the future, but we really can't. It all depends on the next eight, nine hours or so."

33. Ibid.

April said, "It's like God gave him to me and he can't take him back now, please."

Later he admitted, "I had put certain things together that my wife didn't even know about—some pictures and other stuff—that I knew exactly where it was, so if I went back to prison, I could tell her exactly what to get, because I didn't know, I didn't know what to expect."

At the hearing, the District Attorney joined in the MAR. Rabil stated, "Judge, the SBI was able to get a DNA profile of the rapist and killer; that person has been identified as Willard E. Brown. Your Honor, we believe that Darryl Hunt is entitled to complete relief in this case. We move . . . for a dismissal of all charges against him, based upon that."

Before his ruling, Judge Cromer allowed Mrs. Sykes's mother, Mrs. Jefferson, to make a statement. Looking at Darryl, she said, "I understand that nineteen years in prison—if there is a chance that you didn't do it— would be a hard row to hoe. However, I would like the court to know that I do not believe in Mr. Hunt's innocence. And I believe that what you are about to do here today is to set free a guilty man, who is guilty of my daughter's death."

After she took her seat, Darryl was asked if he had anything to say. He stood and, fighting back tears, said:

> "This is hard for me, because for twenty years, I have been trying to prove my innocence. As hard as it is for me, Mrs. Jefferson," Darryl said, turning around toward her in the gallery, "I had nothing to do with your daughter's death; I wasn't involved. I know it's hard, but I've lived with this every day trying to prove my innocence. I can't explain why people say what they say or why they lie or why all this happened, only God can. That's how I lived my days in prison, knowing that only God can bring about justice. I just ask that you and your family know that in my heart . . . that you are in my prayers. Thank you."

Darryl took his seat. The bailiff asked everyone to rise. Judge Cromer announced his ruling:

> Today, we acknowledge that a mistake was made. And, furthermore, with the consent of both parties, we will dismiss this case with prejudice.[34]

---

34. "With prejudice" means that Hunt can never be tried on these charges again.

Darryl listens to Judge Cromer. Credit: © 2004, *Winston-Salem Journal* photo by Ted Richardson

Darryl Hunt is exonerated. Credit: © 2004, *Winston-Salem Journal* photo by Ted Richardson

Afterwards, there was another press conference and celebration at Emmanuel Baptist Church. Summing up his nineteen-year ordeal, Darryl said,

> From Day One I told him [Rabil] that I was innocent and the question has always been, was anyone listening? Today confirmed, finally, that somebody was listening.

five

Making Justice Our Business:
Faith, Justice, and the Work Ahead

Darryl Hunt's release and exoneration set in motion a number of things in Winston-Salem and across North Carolina:

- Mayor Joines and the City Council called for changes in investigative procedures in the Police Department, in order to avoid such tragedies in the future. Chief Linda Davis commissioned an internal study of procedures for conducting lineups for cases involving eye-witnesses.

- Council Member Vivian Burke called for the establishment of a citizen's committee to review what went wrong in the case. The Deborah Sykes Administrative Review Committee began meeting July 2005 and issued its 100-page report, with a 9,000-page appendix, in February 2007. Commenting on material that came to light before and during this review, Mark Rabil asserted that, despite Detective Crump's claim to the contrary, the Winston-Salem Police Department had in fact "never even bothered to check to see if Willard Brown was in prison, when Deborah Sykes was killed."[1] The Police Department

---

1. "If they had even asked his [Brown's] parole officer or probation officer when he got out, they would have found out that he was released in June of 1984. There was a computer record that showed a projected release date of September 1984, but everyone in the criminal justice system knows the difference between a projected release date and

was, then, negligent. If anyone had actually done the due diligence any police officer would know to do, they would have discovered that Brown was at large the morning of Mrs. Sykes's murder. If they knew this, the Police Department was criminally culpable for not having shared that information with the defense.[2] In his Conclusions to this Report, City Manager Lee Garrity, declared "Police Department detectives should have connected the Sykes and Regina K. cases in the spring of 1986 and connected Willard Brown's blood group evidence with that from the Sykes case, in that the same investigator [Carter Crump] was working on both cases at that time." Had that connection and other elements of the case, including the false statements offered by detectives to obtain search warrants, been recognized by the Police Department, Garrity believes that Mrs. Sykes's assailant "would likely have been identified much sooner than 2003."[3]

- Acknowledging that mistakes were made, the Council issued an apology to Hunt on February 19, 2007:

  The Sykes Report reveals actions of City officers and employees, and of others, which fall far short of the standards this city holds and espouses. For such actions by City officers and employees documented in the [City] Manager's Sykes Report findings, the City expresses its sincere regret, extending its profound and sincere apology to Darryl Hunt for all that he has endured and suffered in this matter. The City further expresses its determination to do all in its power to ensure that such a tragic series of events may never happen again.

- In addition, the Council voted to settle the civil suit for $1.65 million filed on behalf of Hunt for his wrongful incarceration.[4]

---

the actual date you get out. Police officers know who to go talk to to find out these things." Stern and Sundberg, *Trials of Darryl Hunt*, 1:27:09–4 3. See chapter 1.

2. As we have noted, in Rabil's view, the Police Department was either "criminal or negligent, but there is no in between and there is no lesser degree." In addition, Rabil maintained, "They covered up the fact that Williard Brown was identified in the Integon [Regina K.] Case. The family of the victim in the rape case has told me that the police basically intimidated her to not prosecute that case. They said, 'Look, it's just your word against his,' which really was false, because she had gotten the knife from the culprit; they had blood samples. They destroyed all that. After Darryl was granted a new trial in 1989, the physical evidence in the Integon Case was destroyed." Stern and Sundberg, *Trials of Darryl Hunt*, 1:27:43ff.

3. Sykes Report, 7.

4. For the major findings of the Sykes Report and the City's apology to Hunt, see:

- The City's Human Relations Commission, led by a white local attorney Hoppy Elliott, called for education, policy changes, and other initiatives to promote racial healing in our community. The Commission worked with Mayor Joines to sponsor several Racial Healing Forums, in which community members asked questions of council members, police officers, prosecutors, and defense attorneys involved in the case.

- On the state level, the Sykes case added fuel to reforms considered by the North Carolina Criminal Justice Study Commission, created by the Chief Justice of the N.C. Supreme Court in 2002. On the Commission's recommendation, the North Carolina General Assembly established the North Carolina Innocence Inquiry Commission in 2006. In short order, the Commission, composed of representatives from the judiciary, law enforcement, the defense bar, prosecutors, victim's advocates, and the public, recommended "state-wide adoption of new laws requiring information sharing with defense counsel, procedural changes in eyewitness identification and what is being called the Hunt Effect— a more alert and critical attitude among jurors—in legal proceedings."[5]

A MIRACULOUS CHAIN OF EVENTS

For many of us, those Advent days leading up to Darryl's release on Wednesday, December 24, 2003, were filled with tension, worry, waiting —and then exhilaration. After Darryl and April left the press conference to go home together for the first time, a group, including Reverends Mendez and Eversley and Imam Khalid Griggs went for lunch. Relieved and exultant, they told stories about the ups and downs of the previous nineteen years. It was a great day, a fitting way—for those of us who were Christian—to celebrate Advent.

We felt we had just experienced a miracle. When all had seemed lost, when it seemed as if there was no way that Darryl would ever be free, when it seemed as if justice would never be done, an unlikely series of events unfolded that no one could have foreseen. They were events

---

www.cityofws.org/Assets/CityOfWS/Documents/Marketing/.../Sykesreportand-settlement_www.pdf.

5. See online: http://darrylhuntproject.org/.

in which a number of people had a hand. A few of the events were co-ordinated, but many were not; all of them were critical to Darryl's re-lease. There were a number of coincidences, or links in a chain, that freed Darryl and led to justice for Deborah Sykes and her family.[6] Here are a few links in that chain:

- Mark Rabil persisted and asked for the virtual needle in the 40,000 DNA profile haystack

- DA Tom Keith agreed and Judge Andy Cromer granted the petition

- Carl Crothers noticed the decision and decided to launch the investigative report

- Phoebe Zerwick read some 20,000 documents and wrote an outstanding newspaper article series

- Mrs. Lane, the mother-in-law of Regina Kellar, called Zerwick and reminded her of the similarities with the Integon rape case

- Zerwick went to the police department and found that Regina K. had identified Willard Brown in a lineup

- Judge Cromer read the newspaper article series and threatened to cite the SBI with contempt

- Anthony Brown's DNA profile happened to be in the state database

- The SBI geneticist, on a hunch, flew the DNA samples from the Sykes rape kit and from Anthony Brown to Alabama

- Though the samples did not completely match, Detective Rowe and Williams, who had been prepared to arrest Anthony Brown, looked at the Integon rape case file and found that Anthony's brother, Willard, had been identified in that case

- Willard Brown happened to be in Forsyth County Jail that weekend

- Whites across the community read the *Journal* newspaper articles, began to doubt the strength of the case against Hunt, and spoke up about it

- Responding to DA Keith's recalcitrance, the Hunt Defense Committee, which now included whites, developed a two-pronged strategy of a white clergy press conference and an African-American press conference

6. Mark Rabil counted some fifty such coincidences.

- Mayor Joines and the City Council called for a review of the case by the State Bureau of Investigation

- Willard Brown, after denying any involvement in the Sykes murder for two days and with everything to lose and nothing to gain, voluntarily confessed to the crime and apologized to Darryl, his family, and the whole community for causing racial division over the last twenty years

This list could be much longer. The point is that there is a fragile thread of events that could have been broken at any point. Had it been broken—had one person not done what he or she did—the case may never have been solved. While Darryl remained in prison, Willard Brown would have remained free and a threat to the community.

The chain of events and its fragility is both awe-inspiring and frightening.

THE WORK OF FAITH

It is awe-inspiring because through the years, so many people—Christians, Jews, Muslims, and non-believers—had had faith in Darryl, each other, the truth or God, and made decisions to act despite discouragement, intimidation, and fear.

In 1984, Darryl rejected the DA's offer of $12,000 and the chance to go home immediately, if he implicated Sammy Mitchell. He didn't want the money if he had to lie to get it. Seven years later, he refused to lie once again—a lie that would have freed him. Instead, he spent twelve more years in prison, believing that sometime, somehow the truth would win out and God would bring justice.

Larry Little had faith in Darryl. When Little first visited him in prison, he declared, "If you did this, I will help them put you away; if you didn't I will fight for you." And he did—in season and out of season. Little talked to police officers, witnesses, community people; recruited Reverends Mendez and Eversley, Imam Griggs, and others to help; raised money; put his house up for Darryl's bail; and went to law school. After every defeat, he got up off the mat and kept fighting.

Mark Rabil—four years out of law school, on his first capital case—believed in Darryl's innocence and simply would not give up. Through two trials, eighteen appeals, the sickness and passing of his wife, and the loss of his private practice, he kept probing and pushing, looking for a way out of the nightmare.

Reverends Mendez and Eversley strategized, organized marches, held press conferences, and raised money. At first, they did it because they had faith in Larry; later, they acted because they had faith in Darryl.

Imam Griggs mentored Darryl in his faith, visited him regularly, and encouraged him to write a journal of how he felt about what he was experiencing.

Countless black community members held bake sales, participated in marches and demonstrations, prayed, wrote letters, and visited Darryl in prison.

Regina Kellar fought, survived, identified Willard Brown's picture, and pressed the police department to find him.

Jo Ann North Goetz, Darryl's white sixth-grade teacher, believed in Darryl and said so to the court in his first trial, despite threats against her.

The predominantly white Forsyth Ministers Fellowship sent the amicus brief on Darryl's behalf before his second trial.

All of these folks "kept hope alive" and did so when many folks in the white community believed the man they were defending was "a rapacious, sodomistic, viciously violent, brutal murderer."

Why? Why did they do it for so long and in the face both of such intransigence in the criminal justice system and of the anger, indifference, or presumption of guilt among whites?

Voicing what impelled him to keep working on the case, Larry Little speaks also for others, particularly those with the Hunt Defense Committee:

> It's like a little old man trying to move a mountain with a shovel, but you try because if you don't, you die. If you give in and let them do this, then essentially you have killed your own spirit; you've killed your own soul—to allow these people to keep a man in jail and you know better. . . . I have a conscience. How do you know that these people are wrong and you just go on with your life? I would go on with my life, but my conscience would come back and say, "But that boy's innocent, still locked up there"; you've got to keep trying you can't give up.[7]

---

7. Stern and Sundberg, *Trials of Darryl Hunt*, 1:14:14–1:15:14.

Once he knew what had happened to Darryl, Little couldn't turn his back and walk away. His conscience wouldn't let him. Others, too, refused to walk away. That was a decision made over and over again by some involved in the case. Those decisions brought pain and suffering to those who made them; they faced ostracism, public censure, discouragement, and, for some, a crisis of faith.

FAITH LOST

At various points in Darryl's long ordeal, it was easy to lose faith and many did. For some that point came with Judge Melzer Morgan's rejection of the request for a new trial after the 1994 DNA exclusion of Darryl and Sammy. The refusal of the U.S. Supreme Court to hear the appeal of that ruling shook others' faith. After graduating from law school, Larry Little, disgusted with the system, gave up the practice of law. Jim Ferguson, who defended Darryl in the second trial and filed several appeals for him, believed that one of "the gravest of injustices" would probably go uncorrected. Reverend Mendez lost faith and considered leaving the ministry for a time.[8] Reverend Eversley admits now that his belief that the jury could not convict Darryl in the first trial reflected a naïve belief in everyone's right to a fair trial, the presumption of innocence, and a jury of one's peers. He learned by bitter experience that that is not true for everyone, especially for a black man accused of murdering a white woman in the South.[9] After Morgan's decision that cost Darryl ten more years of his freedom, Eversley had the following exchange with Larry Little, who had joined his congregation:

> I was devastated, I was in tears. I lost faith at that point . . . . And it was Larry Little . . . [who] is most well-known for founding the only chapter of the Black Panther Party in the South—it's supposed to be leftist, it's supposed to be communistic and therefore atheistic. When I had lost all faith in this whole thing, it was Larry who said to me, "But Carlton, what about the Lord?" And I'm like, "Damn, I'm his pastor; I guess I have to have some faith."

Maintaining faith became very difficult at times for even the most faithful.

8. Asked later what helped him during this time, Mendez pointed to insights gained into the tragic nature of reality from the plays of Euripides and Nikolas Berdyaev's critique of bourgeois materialism.

9. Eversley interview, 2010.

THE ARC BENDS

However, the unlikely series of events that unfolded in late 2003 inspired awe in those close to them, because they suggested that there was a greater purpose, a greater hand at work than anyone could have imagined. Maybe Darryl was right. Back during the strategy session at the IHOP Saturday morning December 20, when Larry Little asked him on the phone what we should do, Darryl—standing at the public phone at Piedmont Correctional Facility in Salisbury, NC—had said, "Larry, let's trust in God. He's led us this far. He'll lead us the rest of the way."

There seems to have been intentionality greater than the sum of all of the purposes and actions taken by the many people involved in this unlikely chain of events. In 1961, Dr. King said, "I am convinced that we shall overcome because the arc of the universe is long but it bends toward justice."[10] In this case, involving Mrs. Sykes, Darryl Hunt, and Willard Brown, the arc was long indeed. Its course traveled through so many twists and turns that no one account, including this one, can describe them all. Yet, when all the doors seemed to be shut and when the light seemed to go out, "a way was made out of no way."[11] Looking back, there does seem to have been a hand holding together this fragile chain of events to lead them toward a just resolution. For some of those involved, that inkling—that realization—left us amazed and grateful. Whether one understands that hand to be that of God, of Allah, of JHWH, or of a moral principle in the fabric of the cosmos, the sense of such a presence helps when all seems lost.

A FRIGHTENING FRAGILITY

The faithful work of so many and the hand of God that seemed to bend the arc of the universe toward justice inspired awe, but it also inspired something else—fear. The miraculous chain of events was frightening, at least to me, because of its fragility.

Two days after Darryl's release, I awoke and was very anxious; I couldn't put my finger on why I felt the way I did. With the help of a friend, I became clear about at least two things that were scaring me.[12]

10. King, "Where Do We Go From Here?" in King and Washington, *Testament of Hope*, 252.

11. Ibid.

12. David Schoeni.

First, I finally realized that what Reverend Mendez and Reverend Eversley had said several times might well be true: that what happened to Darryl could have happened to any one of them—simply because they were African-American. I had never before understood how true that might be. Of course, as public figures and pastors, with more means and connections than Darryl, they would have been able to do more to defend themselves than he had. However, my friend Geoff and his professional parents had been able to do very little to protect him from false charges and even incarceration. As Dr. Angelou had said at an early rally.

> We must remember that Winston-Salem is down South, but New York City is up South. Darryl Hunt exists in San Francisco, in Paris, in London, and you know how many there are in South Africa. A case can be built here on any person founded on lies and hate that can send us to the gas chamber or the electric chair.

It was frightening to think about how "lucky" Darryl had been—if you can call it that. Had several more jurors had a little less doubt about his first conviction, he may have been dead—executed by the state. Had one or more links in what I now know to be a fragile chain of events not taken place, he might have remained in prison for much longer. When he stood up for himself and refused to lie and point the finger at Sammy Mitchell, he was charged with first-degree murder. When he again re-fused to lie and accept the plea bargain prior to his second trial, it cost him twelve more years of his life. Every time he tried honesty, it ended up hurting him. Sometime after his release, I asked Darryl about my grow-ing sense of just how strongly the cards had been stacked against him. He said that for a black man, there are only two credible alibis: "I was in prison" or "I was in a board meeting [of a white-owned corporation]." That would be scary.

Second, as I thought about the series of events that led to Darryl's release, I realized that, however small I thought it was, I had played a role. What I had done didn't seem like very much: I had read the *Journal* series, called white friends to see what they thought, volunteered our help at the Ministers' Conference, met with Larry Little and Rev Eversley, attended the strategy meeting, and called clergy friends to come to the "white" press conference. These things were just things I could do; they weren't difficult; they hadn't cost me very much; they lasted only about six weeks—really only a week, once the events gained momentum in mid-December. But I wondered what would have happened if I hadn't done them. That scared me. I realized that I easily might not have done them. I hadn't even paid attention to this tragedy for eighteen years. Those who had carried the fight were African-Americans; I had felt that it was their fight, their business. I could have continued to assume that.

I knew, though, that when the *Journal* in its Sunday, December 21, 2003, edition covered our press conference and ran a picture of eleven of us, standing in front of Wait Chapel on the campus of Wake Forest University, it had an effect; it played a role. Later, Larry Little told Bob Herbert, the *New York Times* columnist who wrote two columns on these events, that he believed that the press conference by the white clergy made the difference. For him, I think the fact that he could point to at least one group of white people who would publicly protest the sweeping of the new DNA evidence under the rug made a difference. I didn't know then and will never know what difference it made, but I knew on that Friday that it had.

What if I hadn't done what I did? What if I hadn't read the series? What if I hadn't offered to get involved? What if Chris Baumann and I hadn't split up a list of clergy, gotten in our cars at 10:30 Saturday morning, and called people to show up at Wait Chapel at 12:30? What if Richard Groves, Laura Spangler, Lynn Rhoades, Jeff Coppage, Sid Kelly, Fred Horton, John Collins, Susan Parker, Peggy Matthews, and the others hadn't responded? Would Darryl have been freed? I didn't know for sure, but I suspected he might not have been.

That scared me—a lot. Part of me didn't want something I did to be that important. Part of me didn't want a person's life hanging on a decision I made—or could have made differently—on what felt like the spur of the moment. I didn't want to matter that much. I'd rather God just do what needs to be done or that someone else do it. Anyone else. Please.

The effect of what we did also seemed out of proportion to what we had done. Larry Little, Reverends Mendez and Eversley, Imam Griggs, and so many others had worked so hard and faithfully—banged their heads against immovable walls for almost twenty years—and had suffered temporary highs and excruciating disappointments. And then I and other white folks come in at the eleventh, no twelfth hour, and did something that made a significant difference. That didn't seem right; it didn't seem fair. We—I—who had been oblivious for so long—mattered this much? Really? If so, the responsibility to do something seemed even greater, as did the consequences of having not paid attention.

As I look back, an insight from the reflections of Dr. Martin Luther King Jr. helped address the anxiety and the new sense of responsibility I felt. It was something I hadn't understood in his work before these events.

WE ARE NOT ALONE

Though we are responsible for what we decide to do and not do, we are not alone in that responsibility. In this series of events, everyone was necessary; each person's contributions were necessary. No one person could achieve what needed to be done. Although each person's decisions are critical, one person, alone, cannot change what needs to be changed. To repeat, Dr. King said, "We are caught in an inescapable network of mutuality, tied in a single garment of destiny." Thank God. Thank God there are others with skills, insights, perspectives, and opportunities to do the many, many things that needed be done. There were pastors, journalists, mothers, professors, friends, family members, judges, and, yes, in the end, detectives and prosecutors. There were blacks and whites. There were Jews, Muslims, Christians, and non-believers. They all did what they and only they could do from where they were. In the end, it took the contributions of all of these people to free Darryl, to bring to justice the person who had actually murdered Deborah Sykes, to make our streets safer for everyone, and to establish a bit more trust between blacks and whites, who are too often strangers to one another in our community.

The arc of the moral universe did bend toward justice, but not without us—not without our doing what we and only we could do.

On that Saturday morning at the IHOP, when Darryl told Larry Little and, by extension, the rest of us to trust God, he was right. But did that mean we didn't need to make the best plan we could in that moment? No. Did it mean that Judge Cromer, Phoebe Zerwick, Mrs. Lane, the SBI geneticist, Detectives Rowe and Williams, Mayor Joines, Willard Brown, and finally District Attorney Keith didn't need to do what they did? No. We each had to do what we could do. The arc bent—God worked—but not without us—not without each person doing what only she or he could do.

Reflecting on these events, I came also to understand something new in the reflections Dietrich Bonhoeffer said about the work of faith and the work of God. A German pastor and theologian during the Nazi period, Bonhoeffer expressed dismay about the inaction of many fellow Germans in the face of the systematic deportation and extermination of

Jews, Gypsies, gay people, and political opponents. Writing from prison after the Gestapo arrested him for his role in a plot to assassinate Adolf Hitler, Bonhoeffer, who believed deeply in non-violence, reflected why so many good people did nothing to stop Hitler and the Nazi party. He believed that church teachings contributed to the denial of what was happening in the death camps and the lack of civil courage among German Lutherans and Catholics. Those doctrines emphasized the omniscience of God that makes up for the ignorance of human beings; the strength of God that prevails over the weakness of human beings; the righteousness, or justice of God, that overcomes the sin of human beings. In other words, it is all about what God knows and what God does, not about what we know and what we do. In juxtaposition, Bonhoeffer came to affirm:

> We are to find God in what we know, not in what we don't know;
> God wants us to realize his presence, not in unsolved problems but
> in those that are solved . . . . it is his will to be recognized in life,
> and not only when death comes; in health and vigor, and not only
> in suffering; in our activities, and not only in sin.[13]

As our Creator, God has given us the capacity to know, to act, and to create. The expectation is that we will develop those capacities and use them. It's not that we can know everything or do everything; rather, we find God in what we can know and in what we can do. We find God—we experience God—when we focus not so much on what we don't know and can't know, but on what we can know and do know.

Faith, then, is not hoping that God will act so we won't have to, but acting even when we are afraid; even when we don't know if it will do any good or will be enough. It is acting when we can't see what the ultimate outcome might be and even when others may say that this is not your business; a court has decided; a jury has made its verdict; the investigation is over; there is nothing more that can be done. Faith is acting even when you can't see everything clearly and when you don't even know that you are doing the right thing, but you know that this isn't right. You know that if that were you, you'd want someone to do something.

God and our neighbors are not so much interested in what we don't know and can't do as in what we can know and what we *do* do.

---

13. *Letters and Papers from Prison*, 311.

"SOMEBODY WAS LISTENING"

And what needed to be done for and with Darryl? At the press conference on the day of his release, he said, "From Day One I told him [Mark Rabil] that I was innocent and the question has always been, was anyone listening? Today confirmed, finally, that somebody was listening." What Darryl needed was for others to listen to him, to understand him, to know what happened to him, to tell others, and, finally, to do something about it.

We all need that. According to Howard Thurman, the twentieth-century pastor, preacher, and inspiration for Dr. King and others in the Civil Rights Movement, the deepest desire of the human heart and the building block for human society is the "desire to understand others and to be understood by others." When we ignore that desire in others and in ourselves, we turn our lives into "a nightmare" and doom our future on the planet. All of us want and need to be cared for; to be assured that we are not alone but are "the object of another's concern and caring." [14] This kind of caring, or love, requires discipline. Thurman calls it a disciplined use of the imagination that leads to action:

> A man [sic] can send his imagination forth to establish a beach-head in another man's spirit, and from that vantage point so to blend with the other's landscape that what he sees and feels is authentic—that is the great adventure in human relations. But this is not enough. The imagination must report its findings accurately without regard to prejudgments and private or collective fears. But this too is not enough. There must be both a spontaneous and a calculating response to such knowledge which will result in sharing of life and resources at their deepest level. [15]

No matter a person's social location and conditioning, these are things that anyone can do with respect to another and would expect others to do for him or her.

1. Listen to the other and imagine what it would be like to be her or him. This involves an opening of "the heart so that what another is feeling and experiencing can find its way in."

2. Report it. Report what you hear "without regard to prejudgments and private or collective fears."

3. Do something about it, or make ". . . a spontaneous and a calculating

14. See chapter 5, "Reconciliation," 104–5.

15. *Luminous Darkness*, 100.

response to such knowledge which will result in sharing of life and resources at their deepest level."

This kind of love is not primarily a feeling, though feelings are involved. Rather, it is a commitment to act in ways that are just—that is, in ways we would want others to act towards us. At the very beginning, Larry Little went and listened to Darryl, tested what he heard with the facts he gathered, recounted what he learned, and then enlisted others to do the same. He did it because he knew Darryl; he had played basketball with him, and the charges against him seemed out of character for him. Reverends Mendez and Eversley, as well as Imam Griggs, began to listen because they knew Larry Little and trusted him. Still others began to listen because they in turn had faith in Mendez, Eversley, and Griggs.

DISCOMFORT AND HEALING

While not primarily a feeling, loving others in this way involves them; often those feelings include discomfort. Acting—loving—in these ways might not seem right or natural; it may seem strange and even frightening. Those involved in the case throughout the eighteen-year struggle had implicit or explicit accusations directed at them: "Hunt is a rapist and murderer; you are just defending him just because he's black"; "you are interfering with the justice system"; "you're activists who complain about everything." That cannot have felt good.

Feeling strange, unnatural, and even frightened can be particularly the case for those who try to understand what it is like for others who are different from us—for those who seem strange and are strangers to us. In this case, the white people who listened to, reported about, and/or acted on behalf of Darryl experienced distress from external and internal sources. A segment of the white population of Winston-Salem vilified Mark Rabil for years, but he did not let that stop him from trying to get justice for Darryl. Mrs. North Goetz received threats, but she testified anyway. Pastors belonging to the Presbyterian Synod and the Forsyth Ministerial Association risked the ire of colleagues and friends, but filed the amicus brief nevertheless. Heck, I felt frightened just driving over to Emmanuel Baptist; that was eleven years before I even got involved in the effort to free Darryl.

The discomfort, however, gets better; there is healing involved in "establishing a beachhead" in another person's spirit. As Darryl said on the day of his release, "We can all—as one, black, white—everybody can heal from this and grow." I received healing. Several people—Professor Pollard, Reverends Mendez and Eversley, Larry Little—stepped across a threshold—the deep racial divide in our community—and engaged me and other white people. Professor Pollard invited me to see what I hadn't seen in my own community. Reverends Mendez and Eversley demanded justice in Darryl's case and welcomed our participation as we began to find our voices. Larry Little asked for our best thinking and collaboration in what needed to be done.

They were, for me, Good Samaritans; they offered healing. I was blind; I couldn't see the elephant in our city right in front of me—the fact that most African-Americans lived with a very different reality than I did. And, for some eighteen years, I was oblivious to the painful ordeal of Darryl and those who supported him. Since one cannot speak about what one doesn't see, I was both mute when it came to the dynamics that shaped and distorted much of our common life and paralyzed, unable to do anything about them. By stopping to notice me on the road and inviting me to go places I hadn't been and to see what I hadn't seen, Professor Pollard bound up my wounds. He looked beyond my disability and believed that I could see, if I were willing. In doing so, he facilitated my healing. Larry Little, along with Drs. Mendez and Eversley, invited me and others to speak publicly about what we had seen and learned, and to do something about it. By doing so, they helped us find our voices, take up our pallets, and walk. It was by their willingness to engage us strangers that we experienced the miracle of healing. We who had been blind began to see a little better, we who had been mute began to find our voices, and we who had been lame, unmoved and unmoving, began to rise and walk.[16]

They saw, more clearly than I did, the "single garment of destiny" and that injustice anywhere is a threat to justice everywhere; what affects others affects us; what affects us, affects others.[17] Their business is our business; our business is their business, and justice is the business of us all.

However, that garment is in disrepair; there exists a gaping tear that produces a chasm between us and makes strangers of many folks like me and African-American men like Geoff and Darryl.

16. I was directed to this passage and interpretation in a sermon entitled "The Loadedest Question" that George Williamson preached at Wake Forest University, February 24, 2000.

17. King, "Letter from Birmingham Jail," in King and Washington, *Testament of Hope*, 290.

"I DONE GOT USED TO BEING DISCARDED"

Asked for a reaction to Judge Morgan's denial of his appeal based on his 1994 DNA exclusion, Darryl responded, "I done got used to being discarded." He is not alone.

As it turns out, Geoff and Darryl as African-American men are only the tip of a very large iceberg. Michelle Alexander, in her book, *The New Jim Crow: Mass Incarceration in the Age of Colorblindness*, offers some staggering statistics and sobering observations. In the U.S., the prison population has exploded from 300,000 in the early seventies to over 2 million today. We incarcerate our citizens at six to ten times the rate of other industrialized nations. This is remarkable in light of the 1973 recommendation by the National Advisory Commission on Criminal Justice Standards and Goals that "no new institutions for adults should be built and existing institutions for juveniles should be closed." Why? The Commission found that "the prison, the reformatory and the jail have achieved only a shocking record of failure. There is overwhelming evidence that these institutions create crime rather than prevent it." Studies at the time showed that incarceration, rather than deterring nonviolent crime, increased it. Those who had significant "economic and social opportunities were unlikely to commit crimes regardless of the penalty; those who went to prison were far more likely to commit crimes in the future."[18]

For that reason, many mainstream academic criminologists in the 1970s expected that the number of prisons and those incarcerated would most likely decrease in the next decades. Instead, those numbers have more than quintupled.

Alexander observes that there is an unmistakable racial dimension to this rapid expansion. The rate of the incarceration of African-American men is historically unprecedented. For example, in Washington DC three out of four young black men can expect to spend time in prison. There are similar statistics for African-American men across the country. There are more black men involved in the criminal justice system (awaiting trial, in prison, or on parole) than were held in slavery in 1850. More black men cannot vote today than in 1870, when the Fifteenth Amendment made it illegal to deny someone's right to vote because of their race. We

18. Alexander, *New Jim Crow*, 8.

imprison a larger percentage of our black population than South Africa did under Apartheid.[19]

How did this happen? According to Alexander, the War on Drugs, initiated in the early 1980s, fueled the explosion. Though one would expect that incarceration rates would reflect drug-crime rates, they do not. Studies show that people of all races sell drugs at approximately equal rates. In fact, white youth are more likely to break drug laws than black youth. Though there are four times as many white users of illicit drugs than black users (16 million to 3.6 million), more than half of those in state prison for drug charges are black. Although two-thirds of regular crack users are white or Latino, 82 percent of those sentenced in federal court for crack crimes are black. In various parts of the country, black men are sent to prison twenty to fifty times more frequently than white men.[20]

Consequently, many young black men—as many as 80 percent in some major cities—have records for drug crimes—crimes largely ignored when committed by whites. Those records subject these black men to a variety of discriminatory practices—all legal—that are eerily similar to those of the Jim Crow Era. Once convicted, a parolee encounters a "web of laws, regulations, and informal rules" that make it legal for others to discriminate against them in housing and employment, and legal to deny them the right to vote, to serve on juries, and to access public benefits, like Section 8 housing and food stamps. These practices have the effect of marginalizing these men and effectively excluding them from a meaningful place in the economy and the political life of our nation. In addition, a shame-inducing stigma as a criminal, ex-offender, or felon attaches to them, causing further alienation and isolation. These obstacles to re-integration into mainstream society increase pressures on their relationships with partners, children, and other family members. With limited economic opportunities and significant obstacles posed to getting housing and public benefits, crime offers a quick economic payoff and may be viewed as not only tempting but necessary. There is little wonder that recidivism rates are as high as they are.

The War on Drugs and its effects relegate a large population of black men and their families to a segregated and subordinate existence. And it is legal, as were slavery and Jim Crow measures in other eras of U.S. history. If Michelle Alexander is right, and I'm afraid she is, the elephant

19. Ibid., 175.
20. Ibid., 7.

in our nation is the mass segregation and disenfranchisement of African-Americans, particularly men, by means of the harsh criminalization of non-violent drug offenses and the selective and racially biased enforcement of those and other laws. The harm done is not as apparent as the cruel and inhumane treatment under the conditions of slavery and the Jim Crow era; those African-Americans targeted today are, for many of us, out of sight—in prisons and jails or moving in circles we do not frequent—and, therefore, out of mind.

This new form of segregation disrupts the "network of mutuality" in our country. Mass incarceration and its effects constrain the economic and civic opportunities of many African-Americans; they also prove costly to everyone else. For example, high recidivism rates make our streets less safe and increase fear, leading to expenditures on private and public security measures against "the criminal element." To accommodate the 2.3 million fellow citizens now imprisoned requires $55 billion a year—an expense borne mostly by state governments. Further, by incarcerating non-violent offenders, the states and our communities forego from them tax payments, restitution, and child and spousal support.

HOW DO WE MAKE JUSTICE OUR BUSINESS?

As exhilarating and hopeful as the release of Darryl Hunt was in 2003, it did not, of course, put an end to wrongful incarceration or to the seemingly insatiable appetite of the criminal justice system. It also did not make engaging racial "strangers" any less daunting for many of us in Winston-Salem. The systemic, very sobering realities Alexander describes can be overwhelming. How do we make justice our business? What can we do? Can we turn one-time actions into habits? Are there ways to do, as Howard Thurman suggests: to listen and imagine what it is like to be caught in the criminal justice system, to report what we discover about that, and to find ways to exonerate innocent people, to decrease the number of wrongful convictions, and to reduce the number of our fellow citizens caught up in the system?[21]

At the press conference on Christmas Eve 2003, Darryl made several poignant observations about his time in prison. Of his friend, Sammy

21. The Innocence Project, co-directed by Barry C. Scheck and Peter J. Neufeld, is a national litigation and public policy organization working to exonerate the innocent and avoid wrongful convictions. See Online: http://www.innocenceproject.org/fix/What-can-I-do.php

Mitchell, Hunt declared, "No matter what you think of Sammy Mitchell as a person, he is just as innocent as I am." Mitchell was still serving time due to his conviction in the Wilson murder. Speaking to the challenges he and many others—innocent and guilty—face on their release, Hunt said, "If we don't show love to them while they are in prison, we can't expect them to show love for us once they are out." So shortly after his exoneration, Darryl gathered a bi-racial, inter-faith group of friends, advisors, and board members to establish The Darryl Hunt Project for Freedom and Justice. Since its inception in 2005, the Board of Directors has included blacks, whites, Christians, Muslims, women, men, and both professional and working-class people. The mission includes three program goals:

1. to provide assistance to individuals who have been wrongfully incarcerated;

2. to advocate for changes in the justice system so innocent people won't spend time in prison; and

3. to help ex-offenders obtain the skills, guidance, and support they need as they return to life outside the prison system.

With regard to claims of innocence, the Larry Little Innocence Initiative of the Project receives twenty letters per week from prisoners asking that their convictions be overturned. These requests are screened to determine whether the cases meet certain criteria necessary for possible legal action. Students from Winston-Salem State, Wake Forest, and the Institute for Public Engagement serve as interns in the office, reading those letters and referring them to the six Innocence Projects across the state, including Wake Forest's new Innocence and Justice Clinic.

Larry Little speaks at Wake
Forest University. Credit:
©2007 Ken Bennett/WFU

To date, there have been 265 post-conviction exonerations in the United States.[22] Among the primary causes of wrongful convictions are eyewitness misidentification, government misconduct, untruthful informants and snitches, false confessions, and ineffective representation.[23] Among other things Darryl has done since his release, he serves on the Board of Directors of the North Carolina Center on Actual Innocence; as Chair, Client Policy Group, National Legal Aid Defenders Association (Washington DC); and on the Board of the North Carolina Prison Legal Services. To address these problems effectively requires not only the awareness and initiatives of law enforcement officials, prosecutors, defense attorneys, and policy makers, but also the informed support and, at times, challenge of members of the larger community. As we have seen in the Sykes case, public pressure for the arrest and conviction of the perpetrator of this heinous rape and murder contributed, in part, to the momentum that led to Darryl Hunt's wrongful incarceration and allowed Willard Brown to remain free. Depending on the circumstances of the case, police and prosecutors may need time to make sure they have the right person, rather than someone against whom a case can be made; they need public understanding and support in order to do that. There are also times that decisions and actions of police or prosecutors must be challenged publicly. When DNA excluded Darryl, Sammy Mitchell, and Johnny Gray as the rapist in 1994, no person or institution charged with law enforcement or criminal justice—the District Attorney's Office, the Attorney General's Office, the City Council, or its Police Department —re-opened the investigation to find him. There was also not a public demand to do so. As a silent member of the community, I realize now there should have been. By connecting with one of the growing number of local innocence projects, you can learn practical ways to get involved.[24]

22. See online: http://www.innocenceproject.org/Content/Facts_on_PostConviction _DNA_Exonerations.php.

23. Interviewed the day of Hunt's exoneration, former District Attorney, Don Tisdale commented, "If he were tried today under the same set of facts and if you didn't have DNA... would he [Hunt] be convicted? Most of the people who answer that question for me say, 'Yes.' Well, that's scary isn't it? I know that eye [-witness] identification is dangerous . . . everybody knows that . . . in the whole criminal justice system, yet we are tried and we try cases with it all the time. And, if you say yes and, if in fact, he is innocent, that is dangerous. You know, thank God, DNA has come along." Online: http://darrylhunt .journalnow.com/multimedia/exonerated/audio.html.

24. For contact information for state and local projects, see online: http://www .innocencenetwork.org.

In the area of advocacy, the Project focuses on education and reform. We have already seen that the Sykes case contributed to the recommendations of the North Carolina Innocence Inquiry Commission to recommend stronger, state-wide laws requiring more sharing of information with defense attorneys and changes to eyewitness identification procedures. In courtrooms across the state, attorneys and judges are noticing a more alert and critical attitude among jurors, calling it the "Hunt Effect."

Darryl and Mark Rabil have spoken to law schools and university audiences at Harvard, Yale, Princeton, Wake Forest, Colgate, and Widener. Recently, they facilitated a workshop on the importance of police departments not settling for "surface" evidence at the annual conference of the International Association of Police Chiefs in Denver, Colorado.

Mark Rabil, Darryl Hunt, Larry Little, and Tom Keith speak at Wake Forest University. Credit: ©2007 Ken Bennett/WFU

Shortly after his release, Darryl was on a panel with a District Attorney, a Sheriff, and a state Supreme Court Justice discussing a moratorium on the death penalty. A bill had been passed by the North Carolina Senate in 2003 instituting a two-year halt to executions while the accuracy and fairness of convictions was studied. The bill stalled in the House, and there were discussions across the state about the need for the moratorium. In this particular panel discussion, the Supreme Court Justice argued that sometimes mistakes are made at the local level and that innocent people are convicted and sentenced to death.

But, he argued, the problem is the lack of resources at the local level. Darryl responded, "So, because they don't have the money to determine whether someone is really guilty, they kill them anyway?" The Judge said the problem is not in the criminal justice system, but that the people in North Carolina don't want to pay more taxes in order to provide what local law enforcement needs. Darryl responded, "Well, if the majority of the people in North Carolina are for the Death Penalty and the legislature votes for a moratorium, the people, if they really want it, will have to decide they are willing to pay for it." The bill has never come to a vote in the House, but there has been a *de facto* moratorium for the last several years, because the North Carolina Medical Board established a policy in 2007 that would discipline a licensed physician who participated in lethal injections.[25] Adding to concerns about the imposition of the death penalty in the state were revelations during the hearings in the innocence case of Gregory Taylor that the State Bureau of Investigation crime lab forwarded positive tests for blood to the court but failed to present negative follow-up tests. In March 2010, Attorney General Roy Cooper ordered an external review of the lab routinely used by prosecutors in North Carolina. The audit of cases from 1987 to 2003, involving the analysis of blood evidence, revealed 190 cases—three of which led to executions—in which "suspects were charged, but the final lab report omitted evidence that contradicted preliminary tests indicating blood at the scene" of the crime.[26] Cooper fired the director of the lab and has promised reform of policies and procedures at the lab and more transparency. The last execution in North Carolina took place in April 2006.

In addition, in 2009 the legislature passed The Racial Justice Act that prohibits "the seeking or imposing the death penalty on the basis of race." Introduced by Representatives Larry Womble and Earline Parmon, both members of the Hunt Defense Committee, this act provides for a process

25. See onine: http://www.ama-assn.org/amednews/2009/05/18/prsco518.htm. The NC Department of Corrections, whose protocol requires a physician be present at executions, challenged the Board's policy, and the NC Supreme Court ruled 4–3 in May 2009 that the Board had exceeded its authority. Responding to the Court's opinion, Dr. George L. Saunders III, President of the Medical Board, released a statement that said in part, "The Board holds the NC Supreme Court in high esteem. However, I respectfully disagree with the majority opinion. I am heartened by the minority opinion that strongly supports the Medical Board's position." Online: http://www.ncmedboard.org/news/detail/ncmb_president_respectfully_disagrees_with_death_penalty_opinion.

26. See online: http://www.wcnc.com/news/Crime-Lab-mistakes-101224699.html.

by which evidence, including statistics from a particular judicial juris-diction, can be presented that establishes that race was a factor in death penalty cases.[27]

As far as "showing love" in practical ways to those in prison and the 1,200 who are released back into Forsyth County every year, The Hunt Project has developed a comprehensive re-entry initiative, called The Homecomers' Program, that surrounds Associates with people and ser-vices that assist them in finding housing, job readiness, financial literacy, group and individual counseling, and mentoring relationships with other Associates who have already re-integrated into our community. While the recidivism rate for the general population of parolees is 42 percent in our county, the rate for our Associates is 3 percent. This work rebuilds lives and families and makes our communities safer by giving ex-offenders positive, productive alternatives to violence and crime.[28] Since it costs North Carolina on average $28,000 per year to house an inmate, every ex-offender that we help stay out of prison over a five-year period saves the state $140,000. For every ten ex-offenders, this work saves the state $1.4 million. Given our current recidivism rate, the Project could, theo-retically, save NC taxpayers $140 million over five years. I say theoreti-cally, because in its five year existence the Project has served 2,500 of the over 6,000 ex-offenders who have come home. This and other re-entry programs could do more, but are limited in their capacity due to lack of funds for staff, bus passes, temporary housing, and transitional expenses. In 2009, with a budget of $250,000, the Project placed fifty-two Associates in jobs, after they passed job readiness and financial literacy certifications. That's an average cost of $4,800 per Associate and may sound expensive, but compared to the $28,000 it would take to incarcerate an Associate who returns to prison, it is a bargain. It saves $23,000 of public money by help-ing someone find an alternative—$23,000 that can be used for other more constructive purposes. The choice is ours. Will we financially support pro-grams like this that rebuild lives and families and make our communities safer? Or will we spend six times that much to warehouse those fellow citizens who could and do choose to make constructive contributions to our communities when they are given this kind of support?

27. See online: www.ncleg.net/Sessions/2009/Bills/House/PDF/H472v3.pdf.

28. See videos of DHPFJ Associates speaking about the effects of this approach on-line: http://www.youtube.com/watch?v=1HqGpMPUosM.

MAKING JUSTICE OUR BUSINESS

There is a giant tear in our "single garment of destiny." It cannot be repaired from one side only. To mend it will take many, many people—blacks and whites, Latinos, Native-Americans, and Asians; Christians, Jews, Muslims, and non-believers; lay people, policy makers, lawyers, and judges. We need people who will make justice our business. We need those who will take up needle and thread, find people of peace and justice on the other side of the tear, and start sewing toward them.

Bibliography

Alexander, Michelle. *The New Jim Crow: Mass Incarceration in the Age of Colorblindness.* New York: New, 2010.

Bonhoeffer, Dietrich. *Letters and Papers from Prison.* New York: Macmillan, 1967.

Boyd, Stephen Blake. *The Men We Long to Be: Beyond Lonely Warriors and Desperate Lovers.* Cleveland: Pilgrim, 1997.

Boyd, Stephen Blake, W. Merle Longwood, and Mark W. Muesse, editors. *Redeeming Men: Religion and Masculinities.* Louisville: Westminster John Knox, 1996.

Culbertson, Philip Leroy. *The Spirituality of Men: Sixteen Christians Write About Their Faith.* Minneapolis: Fortress, 2002.

"The Darryl Hunt Project for Freedom and Justice." Online: http://www.darrylhuntproject.org/.

Fulkerson, Mary McClintock. *Places of Redemption: Theology for a Worldly Church.* Oxford: Oxford University Press, 2007.

Gura, Les, and Phoebe Zerwick, "New Clues Throw Out Long-Held Theories." *Winston-Salem Journal,* December 24, 2003

Hinton, John. "Evidence Stirs Some Angry Reactions." *Winston-Salem Journal,* December 21, 2003.

"Hunt Trial Testimony." Online: http://darrylhunt.journalnow.com/documents.html.

"The Innocence Network." Online: http://www.innocencenetwork.org/.

"The Innocence Project." Online: : http://www.innocenceproject.org/.

JournalNow Special Report. "Murder, Race, Justice: The State vs. Darryl Hunt." Online: http://darrylhunt .journalnow.com/index.html.

"Kentucky: Department of Public Advocacy—Mistaken Eyewitness." Online: http://dpa .ky.gov/kip/mew.htm.

King, Martin Luther, and James Melvin Washington. *A Testament of Hope: The Essential Writings of Martin Luther King, Jr.* San Francisco: Harper & Row, 1986.

McMillan, Leigh Somerville, and Jo Anne North Goetz. *Long Time Coming: My Life and the Darryl Hunt Lesson.* Bloomington, IN: AuthorHouse, 2007.

"NC Medical Board: Welcome." Online: http://www.ncmedboard.org/news/detail/ncmb_ president _respectfully_disagrees_with_death_penalty_opinion.

O'Reilly, Kevin B. "Amednews: N.C. Court Overturns Ban on Doctor Participation in Executions: May 18, 2009 . . . American Medical News." *American Medical Association - Physicians, Medical Students & Patients (AMA).* Online: http://www.ama-assn.org/amednews/2009/05/18/prsc0518.htm.

Pleck, J. H. "The Gender Role Strain Paradigm: An Update." In *A New Psychology of Men,* edited by R. F. Levant and W. S. Pollack, 11–32. New York: Basic, 1995.

Robertson, Gary D. "Scathing Crime Lab Report Puts Pressure on NC AG. WCNC.com Charlotte." *Charlotte News, Weather, Traffic, Sports WCNC.com.* Online: http://www.wcnc.com/news/Crime-Lab-mistakes-101224699.html.

Stuart, Bryce A. City Manager's Report, Office of the City Manager, Winston-Salem, NC, November 1985.

Sykes Administrative Review Committee Report, Office of the City Manager, Winston-Salem, NC, February 2007.

Stern, Ricki, and Annie Sundberg, directors. *The Trials of Darryl Hunt.* DVD. Break Thru Films, 2006.

Thandeka. *Learning to Be White: Money, Race, and God in America.* New York: Continuum, 1999.

Thurman, Howard. *Disciplines of the Spirit.* New York: Harper & Row, 1963.

———. *The Luminous Darkness: A Personal Interpretation of the Anatomy of Segregation and the Ground of Hope.* Richmond, IN: Friends United, 1989.

Tisdale, Donald. Letter to Chief Masten. October 19, 1984. Online: http://darrylhunt.journalnow.com/documents.html.

———. Letter to Chief Masten, February 6, 1985. Online: http://darrylhunt.journalnow.com/ documents.html.

"YouTube: Darry Hunt Project: Part 1." *YouTube—Broadcast Yourself.* Online: http://www.youtube.com/watch?v=1HqGpMPU0sM.

Wells, G. L., M. Small, S. Penrod, R. Malpass, S. M. Fulero, and C. A. E. Brimacombe. "Eyewitness Identification Procedures: Recommendations for Lineups and Photospreads." *Law and Human Behavior* 22:6 (1998). Cited in Beth Schuster, "Police Lineups: Making Eyewitness Identification More Reliable." *National Institute of Justice Journal* 258 (2007) 3.

Williamson, George. "The Loadedest Question." Sermon delivered at Wake Forest University, Winston-Salem, NC, February 24, 2000.

Wilson, Patrick, and Phoebe Zerwick, "Marked Past: New Suspect in Sykes Case Has Prior Convictions." *Winston-Salem Journal,* December 21, 2003.

Wilson, Patrick, and Michael Hewlett, "DA Defends Handling of New Suspect in Death." *Winston-Salem Journal,* December 22, 2003.

Zerwick, Phoebe. "HE IS FREE: Hunt Gives Thanks to His Supporters." *Winston-Salem Journal,* December 25, 2003.

———. "Keith to Plea for a Hunt Pardon." *Winston-Salem Journal,* February 19, 2004.

———. "Murder, Race, Justice: The State vs. Darryl Hunt." Pts. 1-8, *Winston-Salem Journal,* November 16–23, 2003.

———. "New Suspect in Hunt Case." *Winston-Salem Journal,* December 20, 2003.

———. "New Suspect, New Clues." *Winston-Salem Journal,* December 21, 2003.

———. "Rape Victim Tells Her Story." *Winston-Salem, Journal,* August 6, 2006.

Zerwick Phoebe, and Michael Hewlett. "A REQUEST: Mayor Wants SBI to Handle Probe," *Winston-Salem Journal,* December 23, 2003.

Zerwick, Phoebe, Michael Hewlett, and Paul Garber. "I Always Had Faith," *Winston-Salem Journal,* December 25, 2003.

Making Justice Our Business is the story of Darryl Hunt and of those drawn to him who refused to give up on him, each other, and justice. Boyd tells the story of how one summer morning in 1985, an attractive, white newspaper editor named Deborah Sykes was raped, brutally stabbed, and murdered in a Southern town. A 911 caller gave a false name—Sammy Mitchell—and the investigation quickly focused on him and his friend, Darryl Hunt, a black nineteen-year-old orphan. Facing public pressure and having a history with Mitchell, a District Attorney won a conviction before an all-white jury, sending Hunt to prison for life.

Convinced of his innocence, a handful of people led a community effort to free him that turned into a nineteen-year struggle with a few exhilarating highs, but more discouraging, depressing defeats against an intractable justice system. Their dogged determination led to an improbable series of events in 2003 that broke the case open.

This is the story of an extraordinary man, told by a white, uneasy participant who came late to the struggle but was transformed by the process.

". . . I recommend this book as an important read for every American citizen."
MAYA ANGELOU
author of *I Know Why the Caged Bird Sings*

"Stephen Boyd offers a moving account of the eighteen-year-long nightmare of Darryl Hunt. . . . In the faithful work of extraordinarily ordinary Muslims, Jews, and Christians, we see the force of divine love that wouldn't quit, and we catch a clear vision of what it takes from all of us to create a humane society where it is easier for us to truly love all our brothers and sisters."
SR. HELEN PREJEAN
author of *Dead Man Walking*

" . . . Let this defining volume stand as witness to the fallacy that our justice system reigns supreme; rather, what does is the human spirit that survives and is joined by others equally committed to telling the truth. . . . I am left with an overwhelming sense of awe and gratitude for Darryl's spirit and Professor Boyd's tenacity."
ASHA BANDELE
author of *The Prisoner's Wife*

" . . . *Making Justice Our Business* is equal parts ringing social critique and personal faith journey. For Darryl and for all who continue to suffer unjustly, another necessary blow against the prison industrial complex has been struck."
ALTON B. POLLARD III
Howard University School of Divinity

STEPHEN B. BOYD is the John Allen Easley Professor of Religion at Wake Forest Universit He is the author of *Pilgram Marpeck: His Life and Social Theology* (1992) and *The Men We Lor to Be* (1996).

RELIGION / Ethics

Cover Design by Matthew Stock

www.wipfandstock.com

ISBN 978-1-60899-966-8

Cascade Books
An Imprint of WIPF and STOCK Publishers